Psychic Powers

Psychic Powers

By the Editors of Time-Life Books

TIME-LIFE BOOKS, ALEXANDRIA, VIRGINIA

CONTENTS

Other Ways of Seeing

In the world of everyday existence, the five senses reign, but their powers are sharply limited. We perceive the universe in glimpses through narrow portals, acquiring our knowledge by sight, hearing, smell, taste, and touch. But what if knowledge has wider gateways and thresholds? What if, beyond vision, humans have another way of seeing?

All over the world, from time immemorial, some people have been called gifted with what is known as second sight, the third eye, the sixth sense—powers of the mind that seem to bypass the usual sensory channels and transcend mundane reality. Shamans have communed with their gods, saints have seen visions, oracles have foretold the deaths of kings. And, from time to time, ordinary people have felt a moment's slippage into the inexplicable and uncanny.

Researchers have begun trying to codify psychic experiences. Among the categories posited are clairvoyance, or the ability to see objects and events beyond the range of physical vision; telepathy, the ability to read minds and transmit thoughts; precognition, the ability to perceive future events; and retrocognition, the ability to see into the past. In the following pages, a scientist bears clairvoyant witness to a distant fire, a doctor peers into a vanished past in a moment of retrocognition, a mother hears, telepathically, her child's inaudible cries.

For years, such experiences have been claimed and studied. But they have not, as yet, been fully explained.

A Fire that Raged in a Mind's Eye

On the evening of July 19, 1759, a pleasant party was just beginning at the home of a prominent citizen of Goteborg, Sweden. Suddenly, unaccountably, the most eminent of the sixteen guests—the famed scientist and mystic Emanuel Swedenborg—left and walked outside without explanation. When he returned a short time later, he was pale and shaken. A fire was raging, he said. It had already destroyed a friend's house and now threatened his own.

The guests exchanged startled glances. As they all knew, Swedenborg did not live in Goteborg, but in Stockholm. And Stockholm was almost three hundred miles away.

The party proceeded, but Swedenborg left the house several more times and returned to report the blaze was still spreading. Finally, at 8:00 P.M., he announced that it had been extinguished—only three houses from his own.

By the next morning, a Sunday, Swedenborg's vision was the talk of Goteborg. Had there really been a fire? Or was the seventy-one-year-old's imagination running amok? An apparent answer came the following night when an express messenger arrived from Stockholm with news of a great fire. Three days after the vision, a second messenger brought more details. They matched Swedenborg's account of the blaze and confirmed that it had halted only three doors from his own and had ended, just as he said, at 8:00 P.M.

Swedenborg was a respected engineer, inventor, and author whose intellect encompassed sciences ranging from psychology to zoology. When he was in his late fifties, however, he received what he regarded as a visitation from God. Thereafter, he turned his full attention to theology, metaphysics, and the exploration of his psychic powers, which seemed abundant.

To many parapsychologists, Swedenborg's reported vision of the Stockholm fire is an example of clairvoyance: the ability to see psychically what the eye cannot perceive.

When Past Met Present on a Country Road

Dr. Edward Gibson
…oon, a country physician in England, con-
…dered himself a hardheaded man of science,
…t an experience he had in the early 1930s
…ook his faith in orthodox notions of time.
…ne of Moon's patients was Lord Edward Car-
…n, who lived on the Isle of Thanet. The front
…eps of his house, Cleve Court, led to a semi-
…rcular driveway that opened at either end
…to a country lane. A tall hedge screened the
…ouse from the road.

…Lord Carson was very ill, and Moon saw
…m daily. After one morning's visit, the physi-
…an stood at the head of the steps, deep in
…ought about his patient. As he told the story
…ter, he was not much mindful of his sur-
…oundings when he happened to glance up
…ward the hedge.

…But there was no hedge. Nor did a road lie
…eyond where the hedge should have been.
…y as he might, Moon could not see a single
…miliar landmark. There was only a muddy
…ack stretching across empty fields. Odder
…ill was the man walking up the track toward
…e house. He carried a flintlock and was
…earing breeches, riding boots, a caped over-
…oat, and a top hat with a narrow crown—
…aberdashery long out of fashion—and he ap-
…eared to belong in another century, perhaps
…e late eighteenth or early nineteenth.

…To Moon it seemed the stranger saw him as
…ell. The visitor stopped midstride, and for a
…oment the two men gaped at each other.
…rying to orient himself, Moon turned to see
…hether Cleve Court was still behind him. It
…as, and when he turned again he found the
…ndscape had righted itself. The hedge and
…e road were in their accustomed places, and
…e stranger had vanished.

…Some parapsychologists interpret the doc-
…or's vision as an instance of simultaneous
…etrocognition and precognition. Through a
…ear in the fabric of time, Moon was peering
…to the past—retrocognition. The stranger, if
…deed he saw the doctor, experienced pre-
…ognition—seeing the future.

An Apprehension of Danger

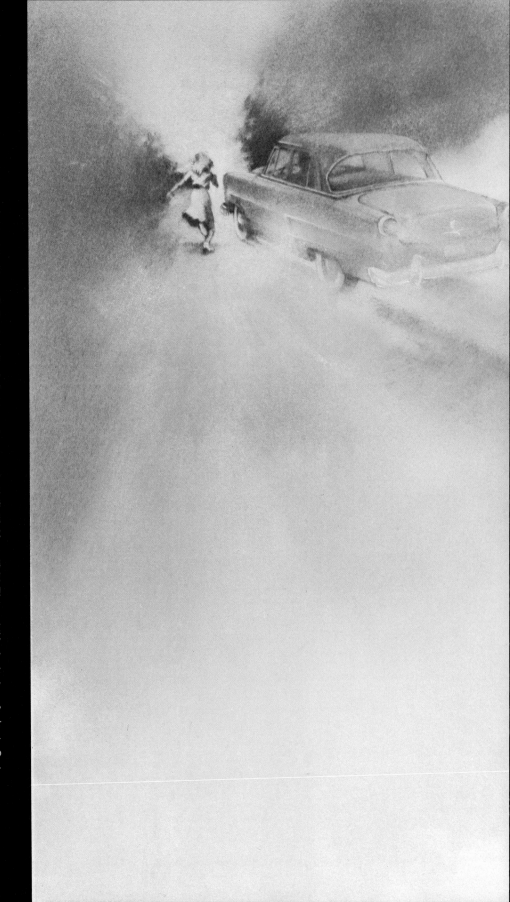

One day in 1955, five-year-old Joicey Hurth of Cedarburg, Wisconsin, came home from a birthday party to find that her father and two brothers had gone to a movie without her. The theater was only a block and a half away, so the little girl dashed out to join them.

Shortly after the child left, her mother, also named Joicey, was washing dishes at the kitchen sink when suddenly, inexplicably, she knew her daughter had been in an accident. Without hesitation, Mrs. Joicey Hurth ran to the telephone and dialed the theater.

"My little girl was on the way to the theater," she told the woman who answered. "She has had an accident. Is she badly hurt?"

"How did you know?" stammered the confused theater employee. "It—the accident—just happened."

Indeed, it turned out that the child, in rushing to join her father and brothers, had run into the path of a moving car just outside the movie house. After being hit, she had bounced off a fender and landed on the pavement, but she was not badly hurt.

"I did not see or have a mental image of a car hitting Joicey," the mother recalled, "but I did have the impression so strongly that I did not question it or hesitate to call the theater."

Recounting the episode some years later, the daughter said that just after she was hit by the car she ran to the side of the street, crying and calling out in her mind, "Mama, Mama, Mama!" She was, she believed, "screaming inaudibly."

Since Mrs. Hurth neither heard nor saw anything that could have alerted her to her daughter's mishap, parapsychologists studying the case attributed her knowledge of it to telepathy—direct mind-to-mind communication occurring without the five senses.

CHAPTER 1

Beyond the Five Senses

I f Samuel Clemens of Hannibal, Missouri, had been content to spend his life as a riverboatman, a remarkable episode in psychic lore would have been lost to history. But his often-autobiographical writings in later years as the author Mark Twain made some of his most personal thoughts public. Among them is the story of a dream he had about his younger brother Henry in 1858.

At that time, Sam Clemens was an apprentice pilot on the steamboat *Pennsylvania,* which plied the Mississippi River between New Orleans and St. Louis. Henry, a likable and handsome lad of about twenty, was a clerk on the same vessel. One night, when the *Pennsylvania* was berthed in St. Louis, Henry stayed on the ship while his older brother lodged at a boardinghouse on shore. Sam dreamed that he saw a metal coffin resting on two chairs in the sitting room, and in the coffin the laid-out body of Henry. On Henry's chest was a bouquet of white flowers with a single crimson flower in the center.

The vision was so vivid that when Sam awoke in the morning he did not realize he had been dreaming. "I dressed and moved toward that door," he wrote in his autobiography, "thinking that I would go in there and have a look at it, but I changed my mind. I thought I could not yet bear to meet my mother." He went out on the street and walked about a block. And then: "It suddenly flashed upon me that there was nothing real about this—it was only a dream."

He told a sister what he had dreamed, but he mentioned nothing of it to Henry on their trip downriver together. In New Orleans, Sam was transferred to the steamboat *Lacey,* which was to head back upriver two days after the *Pennsylvania.* On the night before Henry sailed, Sam got to talking about disasters on the river and what to do in case of accident. "Don't lose your head," he advised his brother. "The passengers will do that!" What Henry should do, he said, was to help the women and children into the lifeboat and then swim to shore himself. On that note the brothers parted, and hours later the *Pennsylvania* sailed.

Two or three days later, when Sam and the *Lacey* reached Greenville, Mississippi, they were greeted at the landing with grim news: "The *Pennsylvania* is blown up just below Memphis, at Ship Island! One hundred and fifty lives lost!" According to that first report, Henry was not among the casualties. But the news got worse as the *Lacey* moved from port to port upriver. By the time

Sam reached Memphis he knew that four of the *Pennsylvania's* eight boilers had exploded, that many of the passengers and crew had been killed outright, and that others had been scalded almost to the point of death. Henry was one of the latter.

Sam found his brother in Memphis and stayed with him until he died. A kind citizen of the city then took Sam in and gave him a bed. Exhausted with grief and strain, he fell into a profound sleep. When he woke, he went to the place where Henry's body lay. It was in a room with several other victims of the explosion, all awaiting burial services.

The coffins provided by the city were of plain white pine—except for Henry's. His youth and beauty had appealed to several ladies of Memphis, who had collected sixty dollars to buy him a special metal coffin. Sam Clemens saw his brother lying exactly as he had seen him in his dream: in an open metal coffin, resting on two chairs. About the only item from his dream that was missing was the bouquet of flowers. As he stood there looking on, an elderly woman entered the room with a large bouquet of white flowers—in the center of which was tucked a single red rose—and placed the bouquet on the dead man's chest. In the most awful sense, Sam's dream had come true. Most people

have never had an experience as searing as Sam Clemens's. But almost everyone has had experiences that are cause for some slight wonder. Someone thinks of a long-lost friend, and moments later that person calls on the telephone. A young man suddenly senses that his favorite uncle is dead, and a telegram arrives with the bad news. A mother writing to her daughter feels a sharp pain in her writing hand, while at the same time her daughter burns her right hand on the stove. A woman dreams of a disaster at sea, and two days later a great liner sinks with hundreds of passengers. A little girl refuses to get on a school bus because she thinks something terrible is going to happen to it, and the bus gets hit at a railroad crossing. How did she know? She just "knew."

It is of course possible to attribute any of these and thousands of similar events to coincidence. Considering how often we dream or sense or just "know" things that do not occur, coincidence no doubt is sometimes the likeliest explanation. And yet, so many instances of apparent knowledge have accumulated throughout history—some of them very difficult to explain away as simple quirks of fate—that millions of people have come to believe humans possess more than five senses. Some additional faculty,

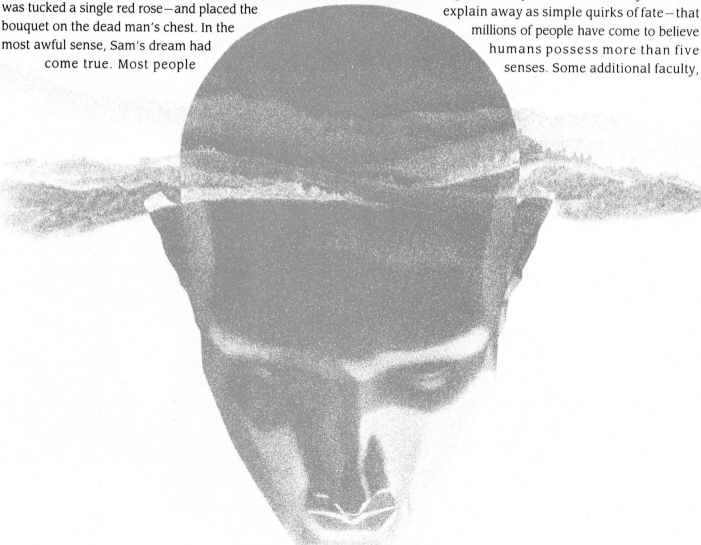

they maintain, enables a person to sense an occurrence before it has happened, or apprehend what is in someone else's mind, or be aware of an event taking place far away. This faculty permits a glimpse into another plane of time or space, unreachable by the ordinary senses of hearing, seeing, touching, tasting, or smelling.

In ancient times, people spoke of prophecies and auguries and miracles. In our more rational age, such things tend to be lumped under the prosaic-sounding heading of extrasensory perception, defined as the apparent reception of information through means other than the known sensory channels. The experiencing individual is said to be psychic.

Three types of alleged extrasensory perception (ESP) are most commonly studied. The most familiar is telepathy, or mind reading, which is the transference of thoughts from one person to another without the use of words. Telepathy is said to occur most often with people—such as identical twins—who are very close to each other emotionally.

Clairvoyance, or second sight, is an awareness of distant objects and events. In its most vivid manifestation it may involve a prolonged vision of a fire or murder taking place a great distance away; more often, it is a quick mental picture of a train wreck or the contents of a sealed envelope or some

A physical resemblance between the young Samuel Clemens and his brother Henry (background) may have been accompanied by a psychic bond. Clemens, later famed as Mark Twain, foresaw his brother's death in a dream.

danger that is creeping up on an unsuspecting loved one. The third type of ESP is precognition, the knowing of something in advance of its happening—whether in a dream such as Mark Twain's or in a waking state, as, for example, the December 1969 prophecy of psychic Malcolm Bessent of London. "Starting with 1972-73," he said, "it will be a crucial year for the U.S.A. Water everywhere, resulting in social upheaval, anarchy, and political confusion. The people will be looking for a new leader, but none forthcoming." Psychics, who often interpret such predictions broadly, see in this statement a foretelling of the Watergate scandal, which preoccupied the American public for two years beginning in 1972. Literal flood did not occur and anarchy is an overstatement; but the entrance of the word "Watergate" into the language to stand for the political upheaval that led to President Richard Nixon's exit from office speaks for itself.

All ESP phenomena, because they seem beyond the limits of our present understanding, are said to be paranormal; serious investigators describe their research field as the science of parapsychology.

Many scientists and other skeptics scoff at ESP research as an extension of old-fashioned

spiritualism—the alleged communicating, through mediums, with the spirits of the dead. Debate continues to rage over whether parapsychology is a true science, a so-called spiritual science, or no science at all. At the same time, the human belief in psychic powers has been with us always, and it remains strong. Surveys such as Gallup polls, academic questionnaires of students and general populations, and random national samplings by various magazines have consistently shown an acceptance of the reality of some psychic phenomena. Often that acceptance is based on personal experience. According to a recent national survey, 67 percent of adult Americans believe they have experienced ESP. The same survey indicated that close to 20 million Americans have undergone profound psychic experiences. It is often said that statistics can be made to prove anything. But there are so many tantalizing indications of something beyond the edge of everyday understanding that it seems unreasonable to brush them all aside as mere fantasy or hallucination or superstition.

People with what appear to be special gifts have lived in every age, and sometimes they have had great influence on the course of history. In ancient Greece, for example, oracles were sought out in times of crisis. Not all oracles were seen as equal, and one truth seeker—Croesus, king of Lydia from 560 to 546 B.C.—put several to a test before making a choice.

Croesus wanted to make war on a neighbor, but not without ascertaining the results ahead of time. According to the historian Herodotus, he sent a messenger to each of seven highly regarded oracles with instructions that on the 100th day after departing Lydia they should ask their respective oracles a question: "What is the King of Lydia doing today?" He did not, however, tell his envoys what he planned to be doing at that time. The messengers duly asked the question and brought their answers back to Croesus. Five of the oracles were nowhere near the mark. The one at Amphiaraus came close but not close enough. And the oracle of Apollo at Delphi answered in verse even before being asked the question. Said the oracle, chewing mulberry leaves and inhaling volcanic fumes:

Lo, on my sense there striketh the smell of a shell-
 covered tortoise,
Boiling now on a fire, with the flesh of a lamb in a
 caldron—
Brass is the vessel below, and brass the cover
 above it.

At the specified time, the king was boiling up a lamb and tortoise stew in a brass pot, an activity that could scarcely have been guessed at through any normal sense. Satisfied that he had found a reliable clairvoyant, Croesus sounded out the Delphic oracle regarding his plans for war. The oracle announced that a great army would be defeated, and again the king was satisfied. Regrettably, he had neglected to ask which army would be the loser, and it turned out to be his own.

When Socrates was on trial and defending himself against charges of heresy, his guiding voice was silent. "How do I explain this?" Socrates asked rhetorically. "Let me tell you: I regard it as approval of what I am saying. The customary sign would surely have opposed me, were I going toward evil rather than good. My approaching end is not happening by chance. I see quite clearly that to die, and thus to be released, will be better for me; and therefore the oracle has given me no sign." So Socrates willingly drank poisonous hemlock, convinced that his prescribed death was ordained by a greater power.

About 2,000 years later, in the Middle Ages, Joan of Arc, the peasant girl of Orleans, claimed to hear inner voices that told her she was divinely appointed to rout the English from French soil and seat the Dauphin—or crown prince—on the throne. The perceptions and predictions she revealed in the course of her short life were as astoundingly accurate as her campaign was brilliant. The English did withdraw, the Dauphin did ascend the throne. In addition, Joan foretold her own imprisonment and subsequent death, saying repeatedly that she would "last but one year or a little more."

In more recent times, any number of well-known figures—the Italian revolutionary patriot Giuseppe Garibaldi, the musicians Charles Camille Saint-Saëns and Robert Schumann, and the inventor Thomas Edison, to name just a few— have experienced psychic episodes. Abraham Lincoln, too, reported paranormal experiences. He believed in omens. According to his close friend and biographer Ward H. Lamon, certain signs assured him that he would rise to power and greatness yet "would be suddenly cut off at the height of his career and the fullness of his fame." Soon after his election as president in 1860, he looked into a mirror and saw a double image of himself. He took it as an image of the future and understood it to mean that he would be elected to a second term but would die before the end of it. After the Cleveland *Plain Dealer* published a story about the president's interest in psychic matters, someone asked Lincoln if the account was true. "The only falsehood in the statement," he replied, "is that the half of it has not been told. This article does not begin to tell the wonderful things I have witnessed."

One he had yet to witness was a precognitive dream, which he later related to Lamon "in a melancholy, meditative mood." In the dream, said Lincoln, he had heard the sound of numbers of people weeping and sobbing as if their hearts would break. He could not see the mourners, so he followed the sound through the White House until he arrived at the East Room. "There," according to his account to Lamon, "was a sickening surprise. Before me was a catafalque on which rested a corpse wrapped in funeral vestments. Around it were stationed soldiers who were acting as guards." Mourners wept and gazed upon the corpse, whose face was covered. " 'Who is dead in the White House?' I demanded of the soldiers. 'The president,' was the answer; 'he was killed by an assassin.' "

As every American schoolchild knows, Lincoln was shot early in his second term by the actor John Wilkes Booth at Ford's Theatre in Washington. Less widely known is the fact that the theater party that night was smaller than had been anticipated because someone else had a premonition, too.

April 13, 1865, was a day of great joy and celebration in Washington. General Ulysses S. Grant had accepted the surrender of Confederate General Robert E. Lee at Appomattox a few days before, ending the Civil War, and was enjoying a brilliant reception given in his honor in the capital. His wife Julia took much pleasure in the festivities.

The next day, however, Mrs. Grant awoke with the sense that she and her husband and child must leave Washington immediately and return to their home in Burlington, New Jersey. She begged Grant to take them away at once. The general had appointments that he could not break, but he promised to leave as soon as possible.

As the day wore on, Julia Grant's sense of urgency increased. At noon a messenger came to the door of her hotel room and said: "Mrs. Lincoln sends me, Madam, with her compliments, to say she will call for you at exactly eight o'clock to go to the theater."

Saint Joan's Voices

A special kind of clairvoyance is called clairaudience --hearing things not perceptible in the ordinary way. Perhaps history's most famous clairaudient was Joan of Arc, depicted above in Antonin Mercie's 1906 sculpture at the Institut Jeanne D'Arc in Orleans, France.

A medieval peasant, Joan lived in a world far less visual than ours. Sound regulated her rural existence: She awoke to a rooster's crowing, was summoned to Mass by church bells, learned news from travelers' tales. Thus it seems natural that what she regarded as divine guidance came to her in voices.

Joan said she first heard the voices when she was thirteen. They belonged, she said, to Saints Michael, Margaret, and Catherine and carried messages from God, directing her destiny and foretelling her future. For example, they said she would lead an army to lift the English siege of Orleans in the spring of 1429 and would be wounded in the battle. The predictions came true.

The voices even assigned her a sword. It would be found buried near the altar of the Church of Saint Catherine at Fierbois, they said. Its blade would be covered with rust, but cleaning would reveal five crosses inscribed on it. At Joan's request, priests of the village church unearthed the sword. It was rusty, but when the priests cleaned it, the five crosses gleamed forth.

In 1431, the English had Joan tried by an ecclesiastical court, which convicted her of witchcraft and heresy. Shortly before her execution, she told her inquisitors of another prophecy from her voices: "Have no care for thy martyrdom; in the end thou shalt come to Paradise."

Almost five hundred years after burning her at the stake, the Church declared Joan a saint.

Mrs. Grant found the man's appearance strange, disliked his manner, and thought his message peremptory. "You may return with my compliments to Mrs. Lincoln," she replied, "and say I regret that as General Grant and I intend leaving the city this afternoon, we will not, therefore, be here to accompany the President and Mrs. Lincoln to the theater." The man persisted: "Madam, the papers announce that General Grant will be with the President tonight at the theater." But Mrs. Grant did not care what the papers said. She felt a growing sense that something sinister was about to befall her husband, and she ordered the messenger to deliver her regrets. When he had left, she sent one imploring note after another to General Grant, saying that they must not go to the theater and entreating him to leave for Burlington that evening. At length the general sent word back to her that he would make every effort to be on time for the evening train.

"I am glad I am going away tonight," Mrs. Grant said cryptically to a friend. "Do you know, I believe there will be an outbreak tonight or soon. I just feel it."

The Grants had reached Philadelphia when they heard the news of the assassination. They learned later that not only had the general been expected to sit in Lincoln's theater box but that he was on the assassin's list of intended victims.

It is not unusual for statesmen to be guided by their own intuition or the intuitive powers of others. Throughout his life, and particularly in wartime, Winston Churchill operated on premonitions that went far beyond hunches. One evening during the Luftwaffe assault on London, the prime minister was hosting a dinner at No. 10 Downing Street when the nightly air raid began. So commonplace was the occurrence that no one thought to interrupt the party—except Churchill, who suddenly rose from the table and went into the kitchen. "Put dinner on a hotplate in the dining room," he instructed the staff and then ordered them all down to the bomb shelter. He rejoined his guests and proceeded with the meal. A few minutes later, a bomb fell on the back of the house, obliterating the kitchen but missing staff and diners altogether.

On another occasion, Churchill visited an antiaircraft battery during a raid. When he returned to his waiting staff car, he walked past the near-side door, which had been opened so that he might occupy his usual seat. He opened the far-side door himself, climbed in, and gave instructions to depart. When the car had driven several blocks, a bomb exploded close to the car and lifted it so precariously onto two wheels that it almost rolled over. Then it righted itself, apparently because of the strategically placed weight of the substantial prime minister. Later, asked by his wife why he had chosen to sit on the other side of the car, Churchill said at first that he did not know. Then he added: "Of course I know. Something said 'Stop!' before I reached the car door held open for me. It then appeared to me that I was told I was meant to open the door on the other side and get in and sit there—and that's what I did." In other words, he just "knew."

Churchill made no known attempt to investigate his own intuitions. But some supposed psychics, and persons close to psychics, have gone to great pains to investigate such phenomena. The novelist Upton Sinclair did—perhaps surprisingly, since more than anything else, he was known as a skeptic and a muckraker. He was aware, too, that there were many cheats and frauds in the field of psychic phenomena. Yet he knew that he himself was not a fraud, and experiences he shared with his wife, Mary Craig Sinclair, known as Craig, convinced him that there are levels of the human mind that are barely tapped. "I say it with all the emphasis I can give to words," he wrote. "There is another and supernormal way of getting knowledge." In his book *Mental Radio,* published in 1930, Sinclair described Craig's psychic talents and the telepathic experiments they undertook together.

Their usual procedure was for Upton, alone in his study with the door shut, to draw a picture of anything that came into his head, and for Craig, in another room several doors away, to attempt to receive the image and draw it. In three years, Craig produced 290 drawings of such projected images as trees, stars, animals, hats, or whatever happened to pop into her husband's head. Once, when they varied the procedure, she received a mental image from her brother-in-law, forty miles away. He drew a simple object selected at random, and she took paper and pencil and wrote down the date and the following words: "Saw a table fork. Nothing else." A day or two later, the drawing and the words were compared, and the drawing made by her brother-in-law was indeed that of a solitary table fork.

Of the 290 drawings, Sinclair rated sixty-five totally successful. Another 155 were partial successes: They contained some elements recognizable from the original drawings. The remaining seventy he ranked as failures. On any mathematical scale of chance, the success rate of these unscientific but earnest experiments may be accounted extraordinary.

In defining what telepathy meant to him and his wife, Sinclair said: "It seems to indicate a common substratum of mind, underlying our individual minds, and which we can learn to tap. We are apparently getting hints of a cosmic consciousness, or cosmic unconsciousness: some kind of mind stuff which is common to us all, and which we can bring into our individual consciousness. Why is it not sensible to think that there may be a universal mind-stuff, just as there is a universal body-stuff, of which we are made, and to which we return?"

Upton Sinclair may or may not have been familiar with the work of Swiss psychologist Carl Gustav Jung, whose *Psychology of the Unconscious* was published in 1916. But he appears to have been groping toward a concept that Jung expressed with considerably more sophistication—and after infinitely more disciplined research. Jung came to psychology through a lifelong exposure to the paranormal, which was accepted as normal in his family. His mother kept a diary of premonitions and what she called odd coincidences, and his grandmother was known in the family for having second sight. When Carl was a student considering a career in surgery, a cousin developed the ability to enter trances in which she said she was communicating with unknown entities. Jung began a lengthy study of the young woman and her circle, ultimately producing a doctoral dissertation on the psychology of the medium. With that, Jung found his calling and the world lost a surgeon.

By 1907, when he met Sigmund Freud, Jung had already published major works on the nature of psychosis and established himself as a pioneer in the psychoanalytic movement founded by Freud. Years later Freud was alleged to have said that if he could live his life over he would go into psychical research, but in 1909, when Jung asked him his opinion of parapsychology, Freud replied: "Bosh." Nevertheless, Jung continued to take paranormal events very seriously.

Jung, in time, developed the theory that he called the collective unconscious. He had noticed, while working with his patients, that certain symbols and motifs—such as the wise old father figure and the evil serpent or dragon—occurred and recurred in their imagery and belief systems. These same themes, he realized, appeared repeatedly in dreams and in the folklore and myths of many cultures. There seemed, in short, to be a common symbolism where no common denominator was apparent—none, that is, but the human psyche. The universality of the symbols led Jung to hypothesize a reservoir of mind matter, consisting of certain key elements of the unconscious, that exists not only in humans but in some sort of continuum beyond the confines of time and space—which the unconscious mind is able to tap. In this framework, he suggested, virtually all aspects of psychic experience could be explained, from odd coincidences and clairvoyance to divination systems such as Tarot cards.

A rumbling from the unconscious might have been behind a momentous incident in the life of Henry James the elder, father of William the philosopher-psychologist and Henry the novelist, who were babies at the time. One evening in 1844 the elder James—a peripatetic American theologian—was relaxing by the fireplace of a rented house near Windsor Forest in England when he was gripped by a sudden and inexplicable fear: "A perfectly insane and abject terror," he wrote, "without ostensible cause, and only to be accounted for, to my perplexed imagination, by some damned shape squatting invisible to me within the precincts of the room, and raying out from this fetid personality influences fatal to life." The experience lasted for a full hour, or so it seemed, and left James in a state of "almost helpless infancy." For years afterward he was dogged by the memory and frequently spoke of it to his children.

In a dream of his own death, Abraham Lincoln stood at the foot of a coffin in the White House and saw a shrouded corpse. Whe

...e asked who had died, a soldier among the shadowy mourners answered: "The president. He was killed by an assassin."

Under the lasting shadow of his father's terror, William James grew to manhood with a profound interest in the strange workings of the human mind. He became convinced that psychic sources supplied "knowledge that cannot be traced to the ordinary sources of information." He sought enlightenment through trance mediums because he believed that sincere practitioners of the medium's art possessed powers beyond the normal senses: specifically, the powers of thought transference and clairvoyance. How these channels of perception worked and what source of information they tapped baffled him. The closest he could come to an understanding of extrasensory perceptions was that they were indicative of "a continuum of cosmic consciousness, against which our individuality builds but individual fences, and into which our several minds plunge as into a mother-sea or reservoir." In this, he was not far from the later speculations of Sinclair and Jung.

Unlike them, however, William James became a leader in the scientific study of psychic phenomena. His interest in objective investigation was sparked by a meeting in 1883 with philosopher Henry Sidgwick, first president of the Society for Psychical Research. The SPR was founded in London in 1882 by a group of prominent individuals. In addition to Sidgwick, its members included the physicists Sir William Barrett, Sir William Crookes, and Sir Oliver Lodge, and philosophers Frederic W. H. Myers and Edmund Gurney. These and other members with equally impeccable credentials set themselves a lofty task: to investigate "the large body of debateable phenomena" consisting of telepathy, clairvoyance, hypnotism and mesmeric trance, apparitions, and hauntings, as well as "the various physical phenomena commonly called Spiritualistic," and attempt to rationalize them in terms of both science and religion. The program much interested William James, who by then was one of the most eminent members of the Harvard faculty. In 1885, he and several other psychologists founded the American Society for Psychical Research in Boston, a group that concentrated on studying the claims of various mediums.

The establishment of these two organizations marked a turning point in parapsychology: Their members were re-

Upton Sinclair's labeled sketch of an ax was drawn and described by his wife after her supposed telepathic perception of it. She claimed to see a "letter A with something long about it" but interpreted the ax itself as a "key or sword" with a similar shape.

Her husband's rendering of a butterfly (above) emerged only sketchily in Mary Craig's versions (right), although Sinclair himself said she got the wings "remarkably well." The round figure below her main drawing appears to be a detail of her larger sketch.

"A diamond set in a stick" was Sinclair's description of the above drawing. His wife transmuted it into a haloed Charlie Chaplin—with whom, she knew, Sinclair had just had lunch. Supposedly, her awareness of this event skewed her telepathic vision.

Sinclair drew a volcano (right); his wife produced a similar picture but called it an upside-down beetle. She sometimes seemed to perceive a shape correctly but misconstrue its sense.

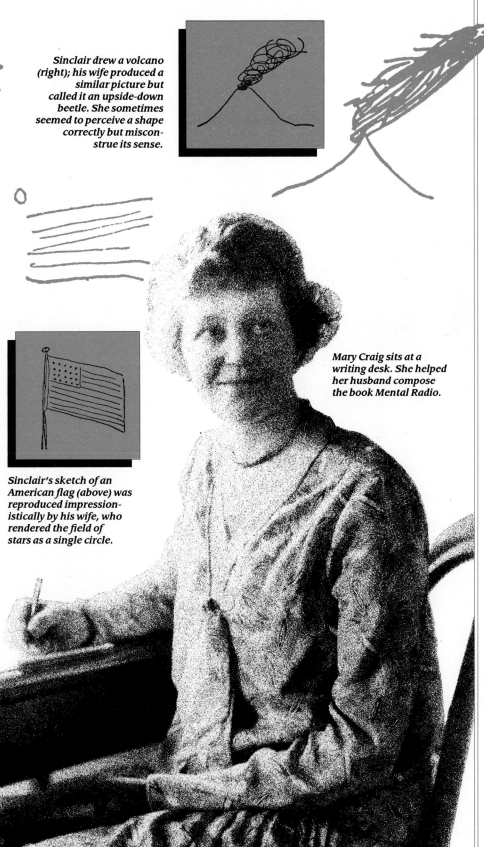

Mary Craig sits at a writing desk. She helped her husband compose the book Mental Radio.

Sinclair's sketch of an American flag (above) was reproduced impressionistically by his wife, who rendered the field of stars as a single circle.

Doorway to the Third Mind

Mary Craig, wife of the novelist Upton Sinclair, believed she had telepathic powers, and in the 1920s she and her husband set out to test them. He would draw pictures and try to transmit them to her mentally; she would draw the image she received. Some examples, from Sinclair's book *Mental Radio,* are shown here.

She believed that while some people are especially gifted, psychic talent can be cultivated by anyone. She recommended a method that combines intense concentration with relaxation. The concentration involves clearing the mind by focusing on a single mental picture. Doing this successfully, she said, produces an almost sleeplike relaxation that is conducive to telepathic reception. The method also requires autosuggestion—consciously carrying into the relaxed state a reminder that the subconscious should be ready to receive mental transmissions.

Although enlisting the subconscious is necessary, she said, that part of the mind is not the source of psychic powers. Rather, such powers flow from a so-called third mind or deep mind beyond the conscious and subconscious.

Sigmund Freud believed that psychic research is a legitimate scientific pursuit but was wary of linking himself with what he had once called the "black tide of mud of occultism." Privately, the founder of psychoanalysis was fascinated by the uncanny and sometimes prone to mystical thinking. In 1905, he saw a man who looked like himself and took the incident as an omen of his own death. He went on to live until 1939.

spected scientists who aimed not to prove the truth of mediums and spiritualism, but to study the paranormal and see if they could explain it. Unfortunately, the investigators in both groups were for the most part amateurs in psychic research; for all their expertise in their own disciplines, they hardly knew how to study so elusive a subject as paranormal phenomena. Right from the start, the society faced difficulties in separating truth from hoax. In 1882, the year of its founding in London, the British SPR undertook to examine a thought-reading act that was popular at the seaside resort of Brighton. The performers were a journalist named Douglas Blackburn and a nineteen-year-old hypnotist named G. A. Smith. The SPR invited the pair to London for a private demonstration.

The team of Smith and Blackburn obliged, not merely for one exhibition but for a long series of experiments during which Smith, as the message recipient, was virtually encapsulated in blindfolds, earplugs, and blankets while Blackburn, the sender, paced the room before the eyes of the SPR investigators and appeared to be concentrating on transmitting a drawing, a number, or some other image supplied to him by the researchers. The results, as published in the society's journal, were amazing. Sometimes the resemblance between the drawings showed no mental connection at all, but Smith's responses were often so close to

the mark that observers believed they might well have been witnessing telepathy at work.

Almost thirty years after the demonstrations, Blackburn charged that the investigators had in fact witnessed something quite different from telepathy. In two articles, *Confessions of a Famous Medium* and *Confessions of a Telepathist,* he asserted that he and his partner had deceived the SPR by exchanging subtle signals. Blackburn claimed to have been astonished by the inability of the society members to perceive and evaluate the evidence that was placed right before their eyes. He wrote: "In describing one of my 'experiments,' they say emphatically, 'In no case did B. touch S., even in the slightest manner.' I touched him eight times, that being the only way in which our code was then worked.

"It is but right to explain," he added, "that at this period neither of us knew or realized the scientific standing and earnest motive of the gentlemen who had approached us. We saw in them only a superior type of the spiritualistic cranks by whom we were daily pestered. Smith and I were genuinely amused, and felt it our duty to show how utterly incompetent were these 'scientific investigators.' Our plan was to bamboozle them thoroughly." In his articles, Blackburn explained how they operated. Smith sat at a table enshrouded in his usual mummylike garb, deaf and blind to the world and sweating under two very heavy blankets. Across the room, one of the SPR members showed Black-

Although he kept an open mind, Albert Einstein considered telepathy unlikely because it seemed to defy physics. Parapsychologists claimed distance between subjects did not affect their telepathic success. For Einstein, this contradicted the observation that forces decline over distance.

burn a drawing that he was to telepathize to "the brain beneath the blankets." Blackburn, keeping well away from Smith, paced the room and studied the drawing, openly copying it several times in order to fix it in his brain. He also drew the design secretly on a cigarette paper.

"By this time I was fairly expert at palming," Blackburn wrote, "and had no difficulty while pacing the room collecting 'rapports' in transferring the cigarette paper to the tube of the brass protector on the pencil I was using. I conveyed to Smith the agreed signal that I was ready by stumbling against the edge of the thick rug near his chair. Next instant he exclaimed, 'I have it.' His right hand came from beneath the blanket, saying, according to the arrangement, 'Where's my pencil?' Immediately I placed mine on the table. He took it, and a long and anxious pause ensued."

During that pause, Smith peeked at the drawing by the dim light of a phosphorescent stone hidden under his blanket. He copied it on a piece of paper while Blackburn sat ten feet away, to all appearances exhausted with the effort of his transmission. When Smith threw off his eye bandage and his blankets five minutes later, he triumphantly produced a drawing that was incredibly like the original, right down to the scale. "It was a splendid copy," Blackburn wrote.

It also was a splendid trick, which he said had been pulled only to demonstrate the incompetence of the SPR investigators — except that the deception was not revealed until the principal figures in the SPR were dead and unable to defend themselves. Blackburn had mistakenly believed that Smith was also dead. However, the very-much-alive Smith responded to Blackburn's confession of 1911 with an emphatic denial that he and his partner had ever cheated. "It was a bona fide experiment," Smith insisted, "and the successful result was either due to chance or telepathy. I think it was most unlikely that it was due to chance."

Like most disputes over which of two parties is telling the truth, this one was never resolved. Skeptics, of course, think it highly improbable that the results were due to telepathy. "The factor which makes psychic phenomena so hard for the scien-

Renowned anthropologist Margaret Mead was a strong proponent of psi research; she said she had observed evidence of "special supernatural powers" in primitive cultures. Risking scorn from many fellow scientists, she helped persuade the American Association for the Advancement of Science to admit the Parapsychological Association as an affiliate.

tific world to accept," Upton Sinclair wrote, "is cheating." But he pointed out in his book *Mental Radio,* "there is no power of man which may not and will not be abused. In spite of all fraud, I am convinced that there are thousands of genuine clairvoyants and psychics."

No one denies that fraud occurs in this as in other fields. Still, the fact remains that seemingly inexplicable things do happen — and they often happen to a good many people at once. On occasion, headline-making disasters have been prophesied by not just one person but by many — psychics and everyday citizens, adults and children, the victims themselves, and those who cared about them. Two notable episodes of alleged mass ESP, each involving a major catastrophe, are particularly compelling. Oddly enough, two fiction writers were among those predicting — with remarkable accuracy — a monumental shipwreck. The first was an English journalist by the name of W. T. Stead, who wrote a fanciful account of the sinking of a great ocean liner in the mid-Atlantic for the *Pall Mall Gazette* in the 1880s. His tale, he said, was intended to prod steamship companies into providing the vessels they manufactured with all possible safety measures, among them adequate numbers of lifeboats. At the end of his fable of disaster, he warned: "This is exactly what might take place, and what will take place, if liners are sent to sea short of boats."

In 1892, Stead wrote another article about a shipwreck,

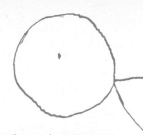

In telepathy experiments in 1882-1883, a bird, a polygon, and a head beneath geometric shapes were images purportedly transmitted by journalist Douglas Blackburn to stage hypnotist G. A. Smith, who then made these sketches.

this time describing an imaginary collision between an ocean liner and an iceberg in the Atlantic. This account was even more graphic. Almost two decades passed, but Stead did not abandon his theme. In 1910, he gave a lecture in which he developed his point about the necessity for sufficient lifeboats, adding a harrowing picture of himself as a shipwreck victim floundering in icy water and calling in vain for help.

By this time, a New York author, Morgan Robertson, had produced a novel about a terrible disaster at sea. Robertson had been a sailor for most of his life, and although he was a natural storyteller, he found the process of writing very difficult. He sat at his desk and waited for the mood to come to him; when it did, he went into a kind of trance, and from there the story seemed to flow through his fingers.

The story that came to Robertson began with the scene of a mid-Atlantic fog on an icy April evening. A great luxury liner, a beauty of a ship, sliced through the murk at twenty-three knots, much too fast for the weather conditions. Its length, he reckoned, was around 800 feet; its top speed was twenty-five knots; and its horsepower, 75,000. Robertson stared at the paper before him. In his mind, the ocean liner drew abreast and passed him, and on its bow he saw the name *Titan*. He saw the lifeboats, also: There were only twenty-four of them, not nearly enough for the ship's enormous size and the some 3,000 people aboard. Ahead, in the fog, the tip of an iceberg showed above the water. "She was the largest craft afloat and the greatest of the works of men," he wrote. "Unsinkable, indestructible, she carried as few boats as would satisfy the laws." And then: "Forty-five-thousand tons—deadweight—rushing through the fog at the rate of fifty feet a second . . . hurled itself at an iceberg . . . nearly 3,000 human voices, raised in agonized screams."

In 1898 Robertson published his novel, *Futility*. A little

more than a decade later, around the time Stead was giving his London audience a vivid word picture of himself as a shipwreck victim, work began on a White Star liner to be called the *Titanic*. She was to be the biggest, sleekest, fastest ship afloat: 882.5 feet long, with a displacement tonnage of 66,000, a top speed of twenty-five knots, and a passenger capacity of 3,000. Also, with a double bottom and sixteen watertight compartments, the ship was designed to be unsinkable.

While the ship was being built, something he could not explain impelled Stead to visit first one psychic and then another. The first, Count Louis Hamon, warned him that there was danger for him at sea and followed up his prediction several months later with a note warning him that "travel would be dangerous in the month of April, 1912." The second psychic, one W. de Kerlor, told Stead that he would go on a trip to America, which Stead at that time had no intention of doing; de Kerlor subsequently dreamed that Stead was "in the midst of a catastrophe on the water," in which more than a thousand people were struggling and crying for help.

At much the same time, an American woman heard a voice which, as she wrote to *Light* magazine, gave her a message about Stead. "The time is soon coming when he will be

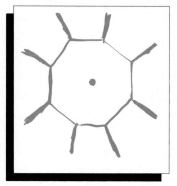

called home," said the voice; "in the first half of 1912." A few months later, when the *Titanic* was in the final stages of construction and looking incredibly like the elegant ship that Robertson had portrayed in his novel, a respected clergyman wrote a letter to Stead, predicting that the

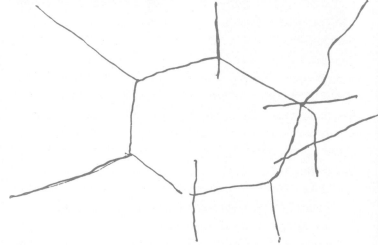

new ocean liner would sink. In spite of these many warnings, including his own unconscious messages to himself, Stead booked passage on the *Titanic's* maiden voyage across the Atlantic, which was scheduled to get under way on April 10, 1912.

Others acted on their premonitions. As the sailing date drew near, a Mr. Colin Macdonald declined the position of second engineer on the *Titanic* because he had a hunch some sort of disaster lay ahead. The banker J. Pierpont Morgan and a number of other ticket holders canceled passage, some of them with the belated excuse that they were superstitious about sailing on a ship's maiden voyage. A London businessman named J. Connon Middleton dreamed, two nights in a row, that he was looking down on the wreck of the *Titanic* and seeing "her passengers and crew swimming around her." Feeling uneasy and oppressed, he told friends and family about his dreams but did not cancel passage to America until a few days later, when he received a cable from New York urging him to delay his journey and take passage on another ship.

On Wednesday, April 10, those who had not canceled were assembled on the decks of the world's most celebrated steamship as she cast off from the Southampton dock. On that same day, a psychic named V. N. Turvey divined that "a great liner would be lost," and in a letter to an acquaintance he predicted that she would sink within two days.

As the *Titanic* steamed majestically past the Isle of Wight, people living along the coast stood on rooftops to watch her passage through an unruffled sea. Jack Marshall and his family, like their neighbors, cheered and waved from the roof of their home, thrilled by the magnificent sight. Then, suddenly,

Mrs. Marshall screamed and grabbed her husband's arm. "It's going to sink!" she cried hysterically. "That ship is going to sink!" In her mind she saw a vivid image of the *Titanic* plunging beneath the waters of the Atlantic and its passengers struggling and dying by the hundreds in the icy sea. "Do something!" she screamed. "Are you so blind that you are going to let them drown? Save them! Save them!" But no one was likely to listen to the ravings of a woman who seemed to have gone suddenly mad.

Four days later, on the evening of April 14, 1912, the *Titanic* entered a thick fog. Nevertheless, she sped ahead at twenty-two and a half knots. The captain had been warned of icebergs in his path, but he thought his ship was invulnerable and he took no heed—not even when the lookout in the crow's nest rang the signal bell and telephoned the bridge. "Iceberg right ahead," the lookout said. It was 11:40 p.m. Moments later, the ship slammed into a floating island of ice.

The blow was a sideswipe that to many of the people on board felt like a minor impact. But the great body of the iceberg struck the starboard side of the ship below the waterline, tearing open and flooding five of the supposedly watertight compartments. Soon, spillover would pour into the rest.

Only gradually did the scope of the disaster become clear. As the Titanic began to list, passengers who had never had a boat drill tried in vain to find places on the lifeboats. Many did not even have that opportunity. They were trapped inside or fell or jumped or were washed into the sea.

For the 2,206 people aboard the *Titanic,* there were a

Voyage of the Titan

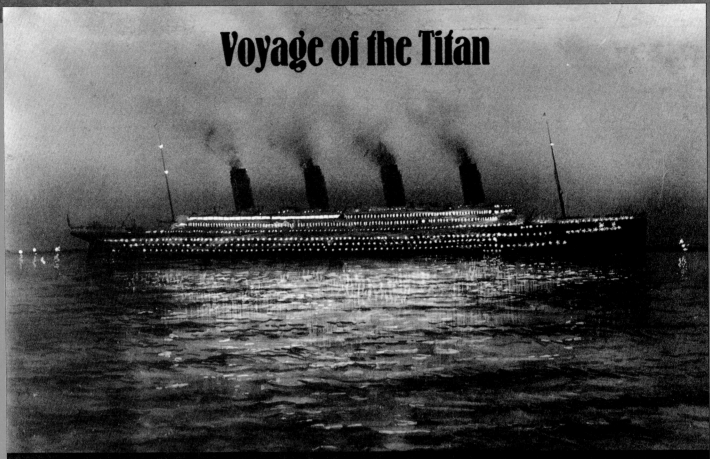

From her fatal maiden voyage in 1912 *(above)* to discovery of her ocean grave in 1985 *(right)*, the *Titanic* has fascinated believers in precognition. In particular, they have pointed to the similarities between the real *Titanic* and a fictional ship, the *Titan,* whose sinking was chronicled in the 1898 novel *Futility.* Believers conclude that author Morgan Robertson had seen a prophetic vision of the *Titanic* disaster fourteen years before the fact.

Certainly, the similarities are uncanny: the names of the ships, their designations as unsinkable and the largest vessels afloat, their collisions with icebergs during April voyages, the high loss of life because each carried too few lifeboats. There were also technical similarities *(chart, right).*

But do these commonalities prove that Robertson foresaw the *Titanic* tragedy? Or is another explanation possible?

Skeptics observe that the names could have been coincidental. Classical literature was better known to readers in Robertson's time than now, so most people would have recognized Titan as one of a giant race of Greek gods. The word had long connoted power and size, and it was singularly apt for a mighty ship.

Technical details, including the watertight compartments that supposedly made the *Titan* and the *Titanic* unsinkable, would have posed no problem for Robertson. He knew ships. Robertson first went to sea as a cabin boy. He spent ten years as a

	Titan	Titanic
Length	800 feet	882.5 feet
Displacement tonnage	45,000	66,000
Propellers	3	3
Masts	2	2
Passenger capacity	3,000	3,000

merchant seaman. Later, he wrote some two hundred seafaring yarns for American and English periodicals.

A favorite nineteenth-century literary theme was society's technological arrogance. Such books as Mary Shelley's *Frankenstein,* in which a doctor trying to create life winds up making a monster, were among the most popular of the time. Robertson adapted the theme to shipbuilders, who, in their race to produce ever bigger and faster vessels, gave short shrift to such practical safety precautions as providing adequate numbers of lifeboats. For the sake of drama, it made good literary sense to Robertson to make his ship the largest afloat.

Collisions between boats and icebergs in the North Atlantic were commonplace at the time that Robertson wrote *Futility* and usually happened in the spring, when icebergs drifted south. Thus April was a plausible month for a fictional sea disaster.

mere twenty lifeboats—with room for no more than 1,178 people. But only about 700 were able to scramble into them before the boats were lowered into the sea. W. T. Stead, splashing hopelessly around in the water among hundreds of others who were struggling and screaming for help, may or may not have had a chance to remember his own warning about what would occur if liners were sent to sea with a shortage of boats. He did not survive to tell.

No one who did survive would ever forget what one described as "the agonizing cries of death from over a thousand throats, the wails and groans of the suffering, the shrieks of the terror-stricken and the awful gaspings for breath of those in the last throes of drowning"—exactly the scene of horror that had been predicted. In all, more than 1,500 lives were lost.

In the decades following the sinking of the supposedly unsinkable ship, many investigators attempted to analyze the multiplicity of premonitions. Discarding all vague forebodings and after-the-fact claims of prescience, at least nineteen impressive cases of precognition through dreams, trances, visions, and voices remained. To be sure, skeptics offered non-psychic explanations for such seeming foreknowledge *(page 30)*. But the uncanny accuracy of the collective predictions suggested to some investigators that a sort of early-warning system, in the form of a central clearinghouse for prophecies and premonitions, might help prevent future disasters or at least reduce their magnitude. Such a central bureau would not materialize until 1967, however, following another cataclysm that had been widely predicted—this time in the little South Wales mining village of Aberfan.

On the morning of October 20, 1966, ten-year-old Eryl Mai Jones woke up at her home in Aberfan and told her mother what she had dreamed during the night. "I dreamed I went to school," she said, "and there was no school there. Something black had come down all over it."

A waking vision of something black had already appeared on October 14 to Alexander Venn, a retired Cunard Line employee and an amateur artist who lived in southwestern England. He kept feeling that some sort of disaster was

Rescue workers search for survivors in the aftermath of the coal-waste avalanche in Aberfan, Wales. Two weeks before the disaster, schoolgirl Eryl Mai Jones (inset) correctly predicted that she and a pair of young friends would die. Two nights before the slide, she dreamed her school was engulfed in "something black."

imminent, something to do with coal dust, and he said to his wife: "Something terrible is going to happen, and it won't be far from here." With a deepening sense of foreboding, he took up his sketch pad and proceeded to draw a human head engulfed in blackness. On Wednesday night, October 19, reported dreams and forebodings began to snowball. An Englishwoman had a dreadful nightmare of suffocating in "deep blackness." Several other people in various parts of England also had frightening dreams of enveloping blackness, and one woman dreamed of a small child running, screaming, from a mountainside that appeared to be flowing downward.

On the evening of Thursday the twentieth, a Mrs. C. Milden of Plymouth, England, was at a spiritualists' meeting when a vision came to her. Strangely enough, it seemed to be on film. She saw a schoolhouse in a valley and a terrified small boy with a long fringe of hair; she saw an avalanche of coal thundering down a mountainside, at the bottom of which a number of rescue workers were digging for bodies under mounds of slag and other debris; and she noticed that one of the workers was wearing an unusual-looking peaked cap.

In the early morning hours of Friday, October 21, a Mrs. Sybil Brown of Brighton, south of London, awoke from a ghastly dream. A child in the confined space of a telephone booth was screaming with fear, while another child walking toward the dreamer was followed by—as Mrs. Brown described it—"a black, billowing mass." At the same time, a London woman woke up from a stifling dream and felt that the walls of her bedroom were caving in on her. An elderly gentleman in northwestern England was puzzled by his dream: He saw, spelled out in dazzling light, the letters *A-B-E-R-F-A-N.*

At shortly after nine o'clock that morning, Eryl Mai Jones joined her classmates at the Pantglas Junior School. Looming overhead was the mountain that dominated the village of Aberfan. Its peak, a 600-foot mass of coal waste from the adjacent mines, glistened with the heavy rains that had fallen over the previous two days.

By 9:14, the morning prayer session was over, and the children were in their classrooms waiting for roll call. At the same time, in an aircraft plant not many miles away, a secretary, Mrs. Monica McBean, was overwhelmed by a sense that "something drastic" was going to happen. A horrible image flashed through her mind: "a black mountain moving and children buried under it."

Above the schoolhouse, the mountain moved. Half a million tons of black waste, dislodged by pounding rain, began to slither, then billow, then thunder down the mountainside in a gathering bulk of blackness that reached forty feet high. Houses were swept away; trees were torn up by their roots; Eryl Mai Jones and more than 100 of her fellow pupils were buried under the suffocating black mass. Pantglas Junior School was gone, obliterated, just as Eryl Mai Jones had dreamed. Rescue workers dug all day and all night to recover the bodies. The final count was 144 dead: twenty-eight adults and 116 children, most of them the schoolmates of Eryl Mai Jones.

During the day of disaster and the weekend, news spread throughout the British Isles and reached people who felt they had known something of it before it happened. Mrs. C. Milden, for instance, saw a television broadcast on Sunday in which she recognized the digging-out operation of her filmlike vision, complete with the terrified small boy with the long fringe of hair and the worker wearing the unusual peaked cap. What she had seen was an apparent preview of the broadcast.

Other predictions surfaced as the days went by, largely because of the efforts of a London psychiatrist named J. C. Barker, who was writing a book about psychic predictions. Wondering if there had been any premonitions of the coal slide, he launched a newspaper appeal to those who might have experienced foreshadowings. Two other organizations undertook similar investigations. The three surveys received a total of 200 replies, seventy-six of which were directed to Dr. Barker—who discarded sixteen that seemed to be obviously suspect and conducted a thorough investigation of the remaining sixty responses.

To more than half of the respondents, the premonitions had occurred in vivid dreams. Most of the others had experienced visions in a drowsy or trancelike state; some, like the retired Cunard employee, had sensed the forthcoming event while fully awake. A total of twenty-four precognitive episodes were attested to either by a letter or diary note written at the time by the respondents or by others who had been told of them before the coal slide.

To Dr. Barker, the evidence he had seen for what he viewed as some kind of seismic sense of impending events was, if far from conclusive, at least suggestive. "I realized," he wrote in a letter published by the London *Medical News-Tribune* on January 20, 1967, "that the time had surely come to call a halt to attempts to prove or disprove precognition. We should instead set about trying to harness and utilize it with a view to preventing future disasters."

To that end, Dr. Barker created an information exchange, called the British Premonitions Bureau, to receive and analyze predictions from recognized psychics and individuals among the general public who just "knew" that something terrible—or even, perhaps, something wonderful—was going to happen. A similar agency, known as the Central Premonitions Registry, was founded in the United States shortly after its British counterpart was formed.

Even the most enthusiastic investigators of psychic phenomena will admit that a great many premonitions do not come true. The hits are remembered; the misses are not. Indeed, there are no reports that any disasters have been averted—or even foreseen—as a result of predictions filed with premonition exchanges. Nevertheless, the paranormal has generated such widespread interest that in some scholarly circles the question is no longer whether it deserves to be studied but instead how the subject may be dealt with in a scientific and rational manner.

Science and the Spirits

The mid-nineteenth century marked one of those historic junctures when faith and reason threatened to run afoul of each other to the detriment of both. The Industrial Revolution had brought with it social upheaval and confusion, as well as a full flood of interest in science. Sometimes old truths withstood the torrent. Sometimes they were swamped. Against this tumultuous backdrop, spiritualism—belief that the dead survive discarnate and, often through mediums, can communicate with the living—raged across America and parts of Europe. Eventually it even came to intrigue the intelligentsia, some of whom saw a rare chance to wed rationalism to belief. What if, they thought, the newest methods of science could be brought to bear on the oldest riddles of metaphysics?

So thinking, eminent Britishers organized the Society for Psychical Research (SPR) in London in 1882. Its agenda included not only mediumship but hypnotism, telepathy, clairvoyance, and any other area where the mind seemed to transcend its boundaries.

An American SPR (ASPR) was organized in Boston some three years later. More fractious than its British counterpart, the ASPR went through several disruptions caused by disputes over aims and methods. Nevertheless, it persists today, headquartered in New York. Recently, the organization began to restructure its jumbled archives and make them available for researchers and historians. From those archives come the pictures on the following pages. They represent some of the earliest steps, stumbling but venturesome, toward documenting the paranormal.

Mental and Physical Mediums

The ASPR compiled massive files on mental medium Leonora Piper (left), host to many spirit guides.

The ASPR studied mediums in two categories: mental and physical. Mental mediums bring only spoken or written messages from the spirits. The more spectacular (if less plausible) physical mediums produce spectral manifestations: rappings, tooting trumpets, trembling tables, and sometimes even ectoplasm — eerily diaphanous matter said by some to be the very substance of materialized spirits.

The society's most fruitful investigation of a mental medium involved a Boston homemaker named Leonora Piper. Piper was discovered by the psychologist William James, who, after early encounters with her, said he believed she had "a power as yet unexplained." Both the ASPR and the SPR probed her work in studies spanning almost thirty years. In all that time, fraud was never proved.

There was much debate as to whether Piper was truly visited by spirits or merely gleaned information from her sitters telepathically. The fact was, however, that she often provided intimate details of their personal lives.

Piper's method was to enter a trance, presumably clearing the way for spirit guides who would speak in voices quite dissimilar to hers. As her career progressed, she could even admit two spirits at once, one who spoke and another who seemingly guided her hand in writing.

A muscular young Neapolitan immigrant named Nino Pecoraro was a physical medium who was studied by both the ASPR and the magazine *Scientific American.* Investigative methods included strip searching Pecoraro, binding his hands, and placing him inside an enclosure. On a nearby table would be such items as a trumpet and a tambourine. During the séance, both instruments might be heard, along with rappings and whistles. The table itself might move. Nevertheless, fingerprints appeared on objects spectrally manipulated in Pecoraro's séances. And once, when the great Houdini tied his bonds, Pecoraro managed only feeble rappings. On the whole, the ASPR found him far less convincing than Piper.

Bound hand and foot, Nino Pecoraro is caged in one variety of the medium's cabinet designed to limit movement (right). ASPR files do not identify his companion.

Antifraud precautions at one Pecoraro séance (left) included swathing the medium in cloth to prevent his helping the spirits produce manifestations.

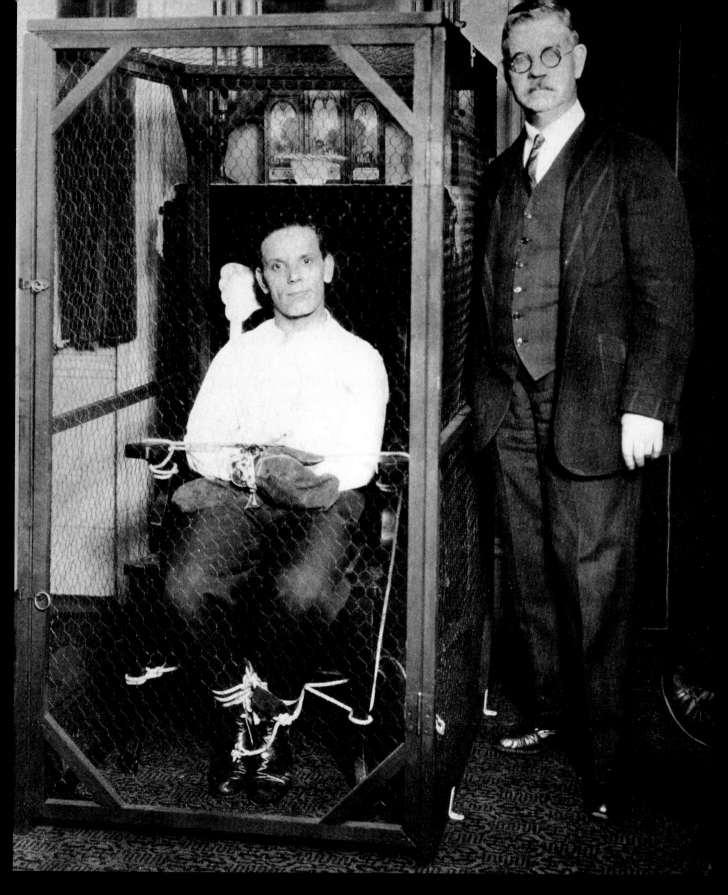

Letters spelling out WALTER appeared on a box during one of Margery's séances.

If not the most convincing, Boston's Mina Crandon was easily the most controversial medium the American Society for Psychical Research ever studied. She was better known as Margery—a *nom de séance* given her by a psychic investigator—and her exploits during the 1920s helped occasion a major rift within the ASPR.

Margery was a physical medium, and ectoplasm was her specialty. Phantom limbs seemed to sprout from her body. Spectral hands groped across tables. Moreover, Margery's ectoplasm was not the usual vaporous stuff but more solid material not unlike custard. Some investigators thought it looked like lung tissue. Margery was married to the eminent surgeon Le Roi Goddard Crandon, who was his wife's biggest booster, but skeptics could only ponder the tissue's possible origin. In any event, she clearly relied on one source of family help: Her chief spirit guide was her dead brother, Walter.

In 1922, a *Scientific American* contest offered $2,500 to any medium who could produce a "visible psychic manifestation," and Margery was an entry. Judges included *Scientific American* associate editor J. Malcolm Bird, ASPR researcher Walter F. Prince, and the magician Houdini. Bird became convinced of Margery's legitimacy and wrote rave reviews in his magazine. Newspapers embellished the story, saying the medium had even stumped Houdini. So incensed by this was Houdini, who had yet to investigate the medium, that he broke off a tour and rushed to Boston. After a few séances, he concluded Margery was an arrant fraud. Prince, who had made his own probe, could not have agreed more. He even suggested snidely that more credulous investigators were being swayed by the lady's personal charms. He and Bird had a bitter falling out, and when Bird joined the ASPR, Prince resigned. He became research officer for a new organization, the Boston Society for Psychic Research. The more scientifically minded ASPR members followed his lead, and the original organization was thus split into warring pro-Margery and anti-Margery factions. The breach healed some years later.

An ill-formed ectoplasmic hand lies on a table before the entranced Margery as she clasps hands with other séance sitters. Walter's hand supposedly frequented her séances, though ASPR records do not specify that this particular hand is his.

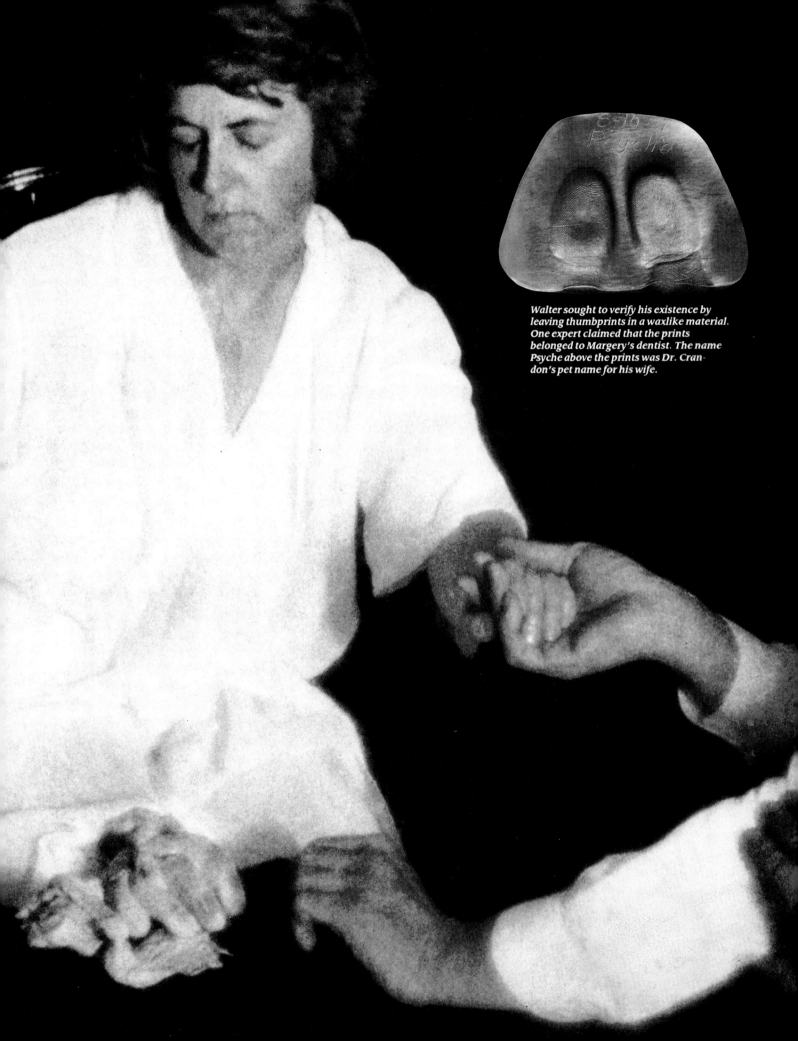

Walter sought to verify his existence by leaving thumbprints in a waxlike material. One expert claimed that the prints belonged to Margery's dentist. The name Psyche above the prints was Dr. Crandon's pet name for his wife.

Ectoplasm: Spirits in the Flesh

Although Margery was a wonder with ectoplasm, she by no means had a corner on the market. In spiritualism's heyday, ectoplasm was all the rage. It was variously semisolid, vaporous, or even liquid, and it might emerge in forms ranging from spidery tendrils to spectacular full-figure manifestations. But it almost always seemed to come from the medium's body, usually emanating from the mouth or some other bodily orifice.

An early and famed extruder of ectoplasm was a Frenchwoman named Marthe Beraud, known in psychic circles as Eva C. Her emanations were said to begin with a flow that resembled thick saliva and end up with a consistency akin to cream cheese. In 1905, Eva astounded the psychic researcher Charles Richet by producing a robed and bearded full figure who identified himself as Bien Boa, a long-dead Hindu. Eva later confessed that Bien Boa was in fact an Arab servant who was very much alive, but Richet would have none of it. He could not have been tricked, he insisted. Eva's confession merely denoted that she was mentally unstable, which, he said, was typical of mediums.

A Canadian medium who went by the name of Mary M. was notable for the human faces that sometimes appeared on the ectoplasm that she extruded. Her ectoplasm was variously described as looking like cotton wool, dough, or paste.

Theories about ectoplasm abounded. Some had it that spirits formed themselves from the substance of the medium's body or soul—or both. Allegedly for this reason, séance etiquette forbade touching the ectoplasm lest the medium be harmed or even killed. Few such casualties were ever reported, however, and violators of the taboo sometimes found that ectoplasm felt very much like cloth. Indeed, one medium who finally declared himself a fraud reported that

The beard was the only aspect of the ectoplasmic Bien Boa (right) that struck investigator Charles Richet as phony.

chiffon was the ectoplasm of choice for him and his colleagues. Sometimes the fabric would be treated with a phosphorescent substance to give it a ghostly glow in the dim light of séance rooms. The material could be manipulated with a variety of mechanical contrivances. Or, it could be concealed inside the medium's body—even swallowed, in some cases—and extruded at will.

This medium survives in ASPR files with a large and detailed manifestation—apparently a bride (right). Ectoplasmic full figures were highly suspect for fraud.

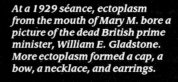

At a 1929 séance, ectoplasm from the mouth of Mary M. bore a picture of the dead British prime minister, William E. Gladstone. More ectoplasm formed a cap, a bow, a necklace, and earrings.

The Astral Pen of Patience Worth

Speech and ectoplasm were not the spirits' only vehicles for visiting the living. In fact, one of the more unusual cases in psychic lore began with a Ouija board.

A St. Louis homemaker named Pearl Curran was fiddling with the board one June night in 1913 when the pointer spelled out: "Oh, why let sorrow steel thy heart? Thy bosom is but its foster-mother, the world its cradle and the loving home its grave." This flowery communiqué was similar to others Curran had received, but the presumed author was still a mystery. In July, however, the spirit gave a name: Patience Worth, born a Quaker in seventeenth-century England. In time, the Ouija board would be discarded in favor of direct mental linkage, but Pearl and Patience would maintain their relationship until Curran's death in 1938.

In early sittings, Patience showed a fondness for aphorisms, but she soon progressed to serious and torrential literary output, dictating plays, dramatic poems, novels. Over the years, most were published, usually to popular and critical acclaim. Meanwhile, the psychic story of Patience became a nationwide sensation.

She was as versatile as she was pro-lific. Although she usually wrote in relatively modern prose, a medieval idyl called *Telka*, published in 1928, was written in an Anglo-Saxon dialect that seemed to date it as pre-thirteenth century. It appeared unlikely that Curran, with little education, was doing such work on her own, though some investigators theorized that Patience might have been a secondary personality born in Curran's subconscious.

In 1924, the Boston SPR's Walter F. Prince investigated Patience, and the skeptical and meticulous researcher was astounded by her abilities. She could, for instance, create two literary works at once, switching between them and never losing track of either. Prince concluded that either Curran's subconscious was working in some radically odd way, or "some cause operating through, but not originating in" her subconscious was at work.

Patience Worth's Ouija-board messages could be considered an extreme form of so-called automatic writing, in which a spirit supposedly guides its host's hand in writing astral messages. A once-popular variation was called slate writing, in which words seemed to appear on a slate without benefit of a human agent. The ASPR tended to dismiss slate writing as more a parlor trick than a psychic event, however, since it could be easily faked.

A psychological explanation for Patience—that she was a dissociated part of Curran's own personality—is also given for a psychic phenomenon known as obsession. An obsessing spirit supposedly invades a person and alters the host's personality. Obsession is considered a possible prelude to spirit possession.

Pearl Curran, through whom Patience Worth allegedly wrote her voluminous works, composed one short story on her own. Perhaps significantly, it tells of a young woman whose boring life expands dramatically when her personality is taken over by a spirit guide.

Dear Julie: Is it almost more than you can realize that I am here? I am glad to come. I want you to become very familiar with this, and then develop and so you. I am investigating and I find it real. It shows that there is no actual separation anywhere. I did not mean to neglect you the other day, but I am so surprised over all things that I can but think of anything. I am out to ... you my sweet girlie. Spirit lives on ever. We are happier here than on earth.

Obsession? The ASPR studied a 1905 case in which the spirit of artist R. Swain Gifford supposedly invaded a slight acquaintance, Frederick Thompson. Soon after the artist died, Thompson quit his work as a silversmith and began painting and drawing obsessively in a style closely akin to Gifford's. Thompson's sketched landscape (right) much resembles Gifford's painting (above).

Phantoms on Film

Generally, the ASPR was dubious of photographs purporting to show spirits of the dead. But when Marguerite Du Pont Lee declared she was taking such pictures, the society paid attention.

Lee, a daughter of the Delaware Du Ponts, was of impeccable lineage, spotless repute, philanthropic impulse, and apparent good sense. Her friend Episcopal minister Kemper Bocock died in 1904. Thereafter, Lee began having episodes

of automatic writing, possibly communications from Bocock. The writing told her to take up photography; she did, usually putting an oil portrait of either herself or Bocock on a chair and taking pictures of it. Some of them showed inexplicable blobs of light and spectral faces, some amorphous, some distinct. Some looked like the dead pastor. About the same time, Lee was having her own picture taken by

William M. Keeler. He was expert in spirit photography, snapping supposed discarnate entities who coalesced around loved ones for portraits. With Keeler's involvement, Bocock's appearances proliferated. There were pictures of Bocock dancing, preaching, sightseeing, and so on.

Lee confided in the ASPR's James H. Hyslop, a philosopher and psychic investigator, in 1919. Declaring that in Lee's case there could be no question of fraud, Hyslop undertook an investigation, only to conclude that he could not say exactly what was going on. But by 1920, Hyslop was dead, Walter F. Prince was the ASPR's head researcher, and the Keeler-Lee pictures had numbered some four thousand. After studying the case himself, Prince had little doubt about the forces at work.

Although deferential to Lee, Prince clearly regarded Keeler as a humbug and an exploitive cad. Prince noted that in all the Bocock photographs, the minister's head appeared facing about one-third off center, right or left, or almost in profile, right or left. The two poses were amazingly like those in the only two extant pictures of Bocock while he was alive. Whatever post-mortem pursuit was pictured, Prince noted, the minister "smiles not, exults not, wonders not, grieves not, nor ever once opens his lips, but is as if fixed in the calm of Buddha forever." Prince also observed that the static Bocock heads were at odds with an alarmingly plastic Bocock body, which appeared variously as fat, thin, short, tall, swan-necked, no-necked. The photos, Prince thought, were obviously faked.

A ghostly face looms atop the ample belly of ASPR leader Richard Hodgson in this deliberately faked turn-of-the-century spirit photograph. Hodgson wanted to show the ease of fraud in spirit photography. Retouching and double exposure were among the more obvious ploys.

Medium A. V. Morgner sits amid a host of spirits in this 1912 photograph. Recognizable shades include Abraham Lincoln at the upper left, and, on the right, Great Britain's Queen Victoria.

The shade of the late Reverend Kemper Bocock dances with the astral essence of Marguerite Du Pont Lee in one of the Keeler-Lee photographs. A skeptical Walter F. Prince commented: "The gown is a bit youthful for the lady, and the head a trifle hypertrophic for the gentleman."

In the town cemetery of Weth-
ersfield, Connecticut, (left) a serpent lies on a grave and a vaporous figure seems to float
above. The 1902 photograph
caused a sensation in the town,
but, in 1920, it was explained
as a double exposure.

A spectral head looms at the
upper left of a deathbed scene
(right). Participants in this
ASPR photograph are unidentified, but such pictures were
common in spiritualist circles.

COPYRIGHT SECURED

A newspaper claimed this photograph of an 1893 Chicago warehouse fire showed victims' spirits in the smoke.

CHAPTER 2

Seeking a Science of ESP

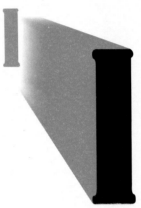

I n the 1920s, most American universities were decidedly lukewarm toward psychic research. At the time, the paranormal was tainted by association with spiritualism and fraudulent mediums. So suspect was the field that a Cornell University psychologist declared he would not even have the journal of the Society for Psychical Research (SPR) in the library lest it "inflame the imaginations and corrupt the minds of the students."

Psychologist William James, an academic of such stature that he could profess an interest in the paranormal and be taken seriously, had died in 1910. In the years following, spiritualism still had enough adherents among the public that Harvard, Stanford, and Clark universities got bequests for psychic research—though the schools were a bit uncomfortable about them. To an inquiry about such activities at Clark, President G. Stanley Hall responded that he "would much prefer to have you use the phrase 'Psychological Research' rather than 'Psychic Research' in connection with the Smith-Battles Fund here, as we do not indulge in what is generally known as psychic research."

What little serious experimentation did go on came to naught. John E. Coover, a psychic-research fellow at Stanford, did a series of painstaking tests in which his subjects tried to guess the number and suit of playing cards held by someone else; he concluded that his subjects showed no evidence of telepathy. At Harvard, L. T. Troland designed a complicated piece of machinery to use instead of cards, but the experiment was more an excuse to try out the apparatus itself than a serious investigation of telepathy. His results were also negative (as he had expected them to be), and, like Coover, he abandoned the field.

If psychic research was to gain a foothold in scientific circles, it needed a new William James—an enthusiast with enough prestige in orthodox academic circles to discourage critics and make responsible psychic experimentation respectable. Just such a figure materialized in the person of William McDougall, a British physician and psychologist who arrived from England in 1920 to take the psychology chair that James had held at Harvard. McDougall had earned enough respect in mainstream science to devise his own curriculum. He was openly interested in the paranormal and would later adapt from the German the term parapsychology for serious explorations in this area.

McDougall used the Harvard funds at his disposal to help launch a number of scholars who would one day make names for themselves. Among them were Gardner Murphy, a Columbia University graduate student who tried inconclusively to send mental images to fellow psychologist René Warcollier in Paris; and George H. Estabrooks, a Harvard graduate student who conducted card-guessing experiments between subjects in separate rooms in Cambridge. But McDougall's most spectacular protégé was Joseph Banks Rhine, an earnest young researcher who was to eclipse McDougall himself and become the father of modern parapsychology.

When he first entered the field, Rhine was as far from the credulous end of the psychic spectrum as one could get. He was a hard-nosed, irascible, skeptical, and meticulous World War I veteran who had enlisted in the Marine Corps despite color blindness and hearing impairment and emerged a national sharpshooting champion. He had grown up in the hills of Pennsylvania, the son of a mother who hoped he would become a preacher, and a father who was a sometime teacher and perennial itinerant farmer. In 1910, after sixteen moves, the Rhines finally settled down in

Marshallville, Ohio, where fifteen-year-old Joseph took a liking to a nineteen-year-old teacher named Louisa Weckesser, whom he married when he returned home from World War I. The two of them immediately went to the University of Chicago in order to study botany.

When the Rhines arrived in Chicago, a titanic clash between science and religion was in full force. Charles Darwin's theory of evolution had been accepted by most intellectuals, and the proposition that humans were descended from apelike creatures rather than from Adam and Eve was seen as a grave challenge to the authority of the Bible. Many people were also disturbed by the new school of behaviorist psychology, which seemed to reduce human free will to a series of programmed responses to changing environmental stimuli. One popular spokesman for that mechanistic view, John Watson, insisted that people were just complicated rats.

Although Joseph Rhine was impatient with traditional theology, he also recognized zealous fundamentalism in science when he saw it; he refused to follow Watson. Instead, Rhine began to wonder whether scientific methodologies such as those he and his wife used in the study of plants could be applied to territories of the mind

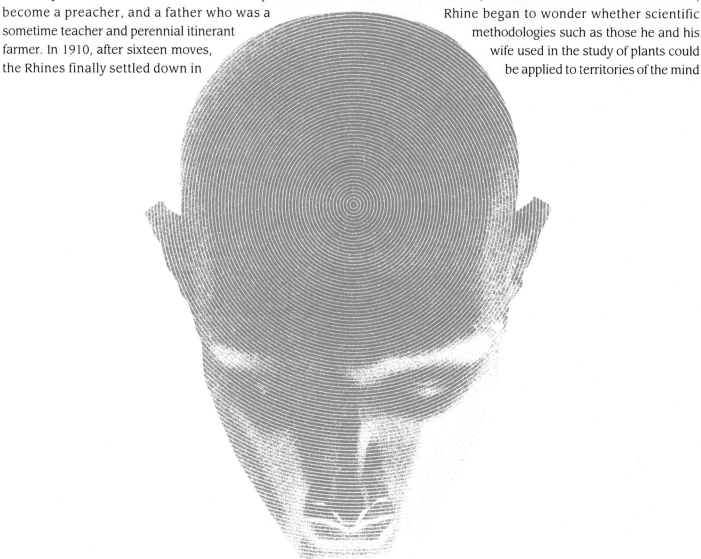

that until then had been the sole property of religion or had been accepted on faith.

Rhine was galvanized into action in May 1922 when he went to a lecture given in Chicago by Sir Arthur Conan Doyle, at the time almost as well known for his dabbling in spiritualism as for his famous detective, Sherlock Holmes. The young botanist was impressed by Conan Doyle, and he was even more taken with the names of famous scientists said by Conan Doyle to share the conviction that some kind of reality exists beyond the material world. One of these scientists was Sir Oliver Lodge, an eminent British physicist. Rhine read his book, *The Survival of Man,* in which the author claimed to have communicated with his dead son through Gladys Osborne Leonard, a well-known British medium.

The book changed Rhine's life. Here was a scientist of international repute, proudly proclaiming a belief in life after death. And if Rhine was heartened by such credentials, he was even more pleased with his reading of McDougall's *Body and Mind,* which argued that psychic research was needed to complete a full picture of human nature. Rhine concluded that it would be "unpardonable for the scientific world today to overlook evidences of the supernormal in the world—if there are such."

In the summer of 1926, Rhine abandoned botany altogether and went with Louisa to Boston, lured by the prospect of meeting McDougall and associating with the Boston contingent of the American Society for Psychical Research. He could not have had a more unpropitious beginning. McDougall left for Europe on the day Rhine went to meet him, and the Harvard research funds Rhine hoped for were impossible to get. The closest he and Louisa came to psychic exploration was a sitting with Mina Crandon, known as Margery, who was hailed by Beacon Hill psychic enthusiasts as a medium of remarkable abilities. The wife of a respected Boston surgeon, she was said to have called up any number of spirits.

The séance took place after a dinner party at the Crandons' home. The participants were told that Margery would summon the spirit of her dead brother, Walter, who had been killed in a freak railroad accident. Rhine was seated next to Margery, and he noticed that although she was tied to her chair as if to keep her from cheating, her bonds were quite loose. The lights were extinguished, and Margery swooned into what appeared to be a trance. While the other guests were marveling at the disembodied antics of Walter's alleged ghost, who played music, rang bells, and bantered with the guests, Rhine grew more and more suspicious that the effects were being manipulated by the supposedly unconscious Margery. He was convinced he was right when he saw Margery kicking a megaphone within reach of her bound hands so that she could use it to project Walter's voice to her credulous audience.

In a word, Margery was a fake. Rhine exposed her in a letter to the ASPR, saying of her performance: "We could not help but see the falseness of it all." Instead of enhancing his own reputation, the only effect of Rhine's letter was to alienate him from the psychic organizations on both sides of the Atlantic. Sir Arthur Conan Doyle even went so far as to pay for a black-bordered advertisement in a Boston newspaper: "J. B. Rhine," said the ad, "is a monumental ass."

The experience with Margery led Rhine to a far-reaching conclusion. Even barring fraud, he decided, all anecdotes of psychic phenomena "happen and are gone, leaving nothing but memory, none of the hard reality of a meteorite or a fossil." The way to study the psychic abilities that so intrigued him would be controlled experimentation demonstrating the same effects again and again.

Rhine got his chance to develop such experiments a year later, when McDougall, back from Europe, accepted what he called a "gilded offer" to create a psychology department at Duke University in Durham, North Carolina. Impressed by his young colleague, McDougall invited Rhine to join him there and undertake psychic research. By 1930, Rhine was developing the techniques that would usher in a new era of study.

He began with experiments in which he asked subjects to guess the order of a shuffled deck of cards. If they scored better than could be expected by chance, it was reasonable to assume that some unknown factor was operating. At first Rhine, like his predecessors, used standard decks of fifty-two

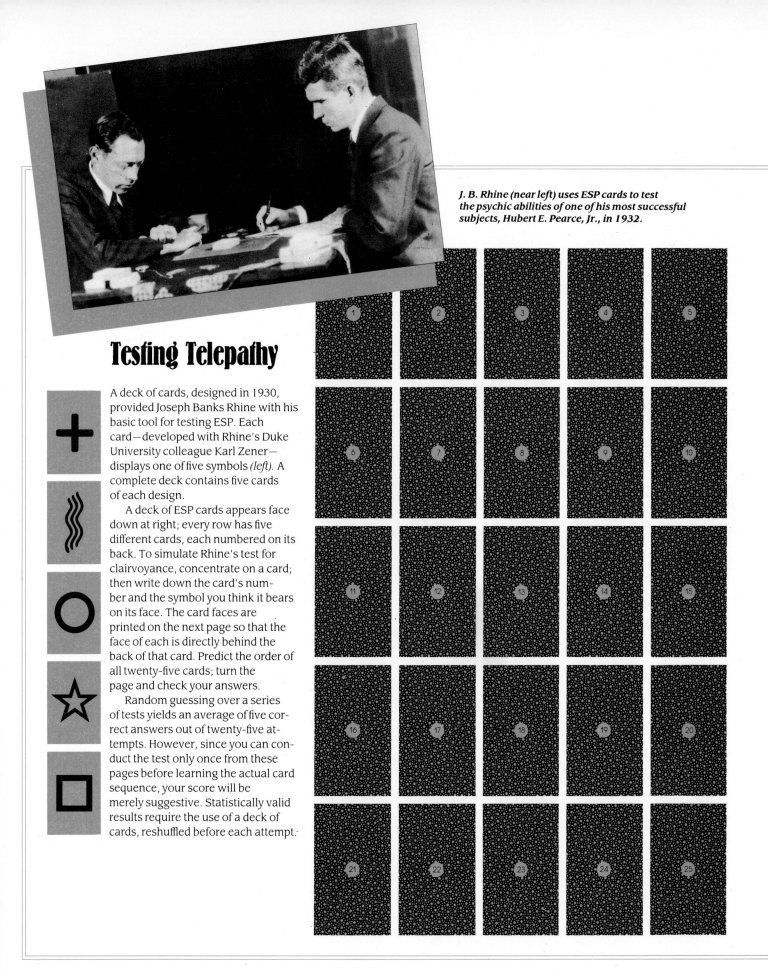

Testing Telepathy

A deck of cards, designed in 1930, provided Joseph Banks Rhine with his basic tool for testing ESP. Each card—developed with Rhine's Duke University colleague Karl Zener—displays one of five symbols *(left)*. A complete deck contains five cards of each design.

A deck of ESP cards appears face down at right; every row has five different cards, each numbered on its back. To simulate Rhine's test for clairvoyance, concentrate on a card; then write down the card's number and the symbol you think it bears on its face. The card faces are printed on the next page so that the face of each is directly behind the back of that card. Predict the order of all twenty-five cards; turn the page and check your answers.

Random guessing over a series of tests yields an average of five correct answers out of twenty-five attempts. However, since you can conduct the test only once from these pages before learning the actual card sequence, your score will be merely suggestive. Statistically valid results require the use of a deck of cards, reshuffled before each attempt.

playing cards. But after a few unsatisfying attempts to prove anything, he decided that fifty-two was too large a number and might lead subjects into habits and superstitions—guessing their favorite cards or avoiding bad-luck ones.

To bar distractions such as these, Rhine persuaded one of his colleagues, Karl Zener, who was an expert in the psychology of perception, to design a set of five cards, each with a spare and unambiguous design on it. Zener obliged with a set that contained a plus sign, a circle, a square, a star, and a wavy line *(below)*. Rhine christened them Zener cards.

In order to check your answers to the test on the preceding page, you should compare the number of each card and the symbol you predicted to the corresponding card in the deck pictured below. Note that the cards are numbered from right to left.

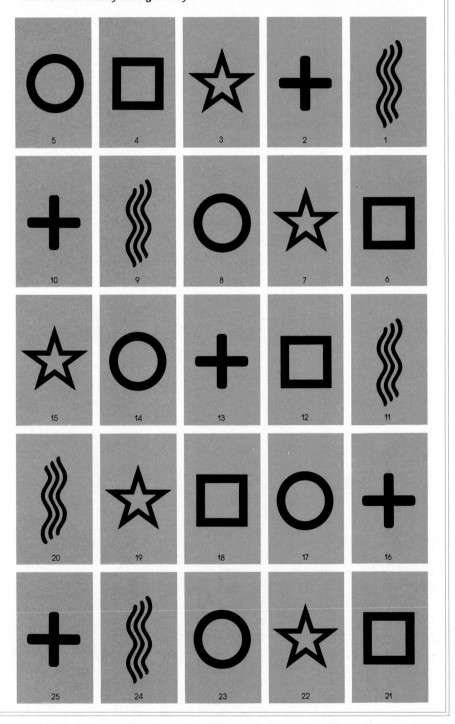

The conception of the Zener card experiments was simple. In a pack of twenty-five cards containing five cards of each design, chance decreed that any person would be expected to guess five of the cards correctly. Each correct guess was called a hit. True, somebody might hit one or two, more or less, in any given twenty-five-card pack, but over many trials with many packs, the law of averages would bring the guesser's average closer to five—unless something other than the law of averages was at work.

For more than a year, Rhine and several colleagues searched tirelessly for someone who showed outstanding talent for picking Zener cards. In the spring of 1931, they hit pay dirt in one Adam J. Linzmayer—an economics student who had achieved high scores in three trials running. Standing across the room from Linzmayer one afternoon, with his spare hand shielding the deck, Rhine peeked at the top card and asked Linzmayer what it was. Linzmayer guessed correctly. He guessed the next one too—and the next, and the next, and the next—until he had hit nine in a row against odds of two million to one.

Rhine was ecstatic. The next day, he dragged Linzmayer back into the lab, and Linzmayer did it again. Nine in a row. All correct. He then continued to guess through a stack of 300 cards, hitting 119, almost twice what chance would have yielded. For two years, Rhine worked with Linzmayer on these and other experiments; however, Linzmayer's scores gradually crept down to just about the level of chance. Meanwhile, Rhine undertook a long, frustrating search for new psychic talent. He found it in 1932, in a shy divinity student named Hubert E. Pearce, Jr. Pearce first displayed extraordinary powers with Zener exercises in which he shuffled his own deck and guessed each card before turning it over. His scores of more than ten hits per twenty-five cards were remarkable. Rhine, anticipating accusations of fraud if Pearce touched the cards, designed an experiment with his assistant, Joseph Gaither Pratt, that still ranks among the most impressive demonstrations of supposed ESP.

Pearce sat in the Duke library while Pratt sat with paper and pencil in the physics building, 100 yards away. Pearce and Pratt synchronized their watches, and at a prearranged time, Pratt picked the top card off a Zener deck and placed it face down on the table without looking at it. There it lay for one minute while Pearce wrote down his guess; then Pratt picked up another card. When he was finished with the deck, Pratt would turn the cards over one by one to record the order before shuffling and starting again. At the end of each session, Pearce and Pratt would each seal their records and hand them over to Rhine before meeting to evaluate their copies.

The results were astonishing, even to Rhine. According to Pratt's records Pearce went through twelve runs of the Zener deck, scoring as high as thirteen hits per run and averaging 261 out of 750 cards, against odds of nearly ten hits.

In addition to placing Pearce's abilities firmly outside the realm of coincidence, the Pearce-Pratt experiments suggested to parapsychologists that psychic ability was not limited by distance. Pratt tested Pearce while sitting in another building 250 yards from the library, with much the same results. Subsequent experiments, in which Pearce guessed the approximate order of a deck even before it was shuffled, suggested his abilities were not limited by time either.

The Duke team designed other experiments in hopes of distinguishing clairvoyance (the perception of unseen objects or events) from telepathy (the grasping of another's thoughts). In one exercise, called BT (Before Touching), subjects would look at a card face down, record a guess, and then turn up the card to see if they had made a hit. In another, called DT (Down Through), subjects simply guessed the order of a pack of cards without touching them. In both cases, since there was no other mind actively involved, clairvoyance was said to have been demonstrated if better-than-chance scores were achieved. To search for PT (Pure Telepathy), Rhine would have an "agent" imagine a certain card while the "receiver" would try to guess the one being imagined.

Rhine and his associates had no explanations for the results, but they did begin to discern what they saw as a psychology of the psychic process. They found that mood affected apparent psychic abilities: Subjects generally did better when they were encouraged or challenged. On one memorable occasion, Rhine offered Pearce $100 for every hit, and Pearce won $2,500 in a twenty-five-card streak at odds of 298,023,223,876,953,125 to 1. Conversely, people tended to do worse when they were tired, bored, self-conscious, or depressed. Pearce's scores, for example, declined considerably after his fiancée jilted him.

In addition to individual motivational factors, there was a general tendency of ESP scores to drop—often to chance levels—over prolonged bouts of testing. This trend, dubbed the decline effect, had been observed by psychic investigators long before Rhine. Skeptics claimed the decline effect as evidence that ESP does not exist and that declining scores were the result of better experimental controls. But Rhine was quick to point out that similar declines occurred in other experiments involving motivation. If ESP behaved like other psychological phenomena, he maintained, then the probability increased that it was a naturally occurring human attribute.

Nevertheless, Rhine sought various ways to combat the decline effect. One harrowing night, he fed Linzmayer a triple dose of the supposedly harmless barbiturate sodium amytal, a depressant, to see if it would affect his scores. Linzmayer fell into a stupor, and Rhine had to drag him back to his room under cover of darkness to avoid unsavory publicity. In a later test with caffeine, Pearce's powers seemed to improve.

Naturally cautious and always conscious of lurking critics, Rhine kept his work at Duke quiet until he was ready to make a clear-cut case for it. After three years of research and 100,000 individual tests, Rhine went public, disclosing his findings in a monograph published in 1934. For its title, he invented the term extrasensory perception—ESP. He told a friend that he wanted "to make it sound as normal as maybe." Perception was an established subject of psychology by that time, and Rhine hoped psychologists would recognize ESP as a branch of perception, rather than as some otherworldly, nonprofessional pastime.

Extra-Sensory Perception eventually reached millions of readers, an enormous audience for a scholarly treatise. The press knew from the heyday of spiritualism that the public loves news of the paranormal, and so they made the most of it. Certain reporters at the *New York Times,* the New York *Herald Tribune,* and *Scientific American* took to specializing in the area, maintaining the public's interest in ESP for years after the book was released.

Even in the academic world, *Extra-Sensory Perception* was hailed as "epoch making." By demonstrating consistent results, Rhine overcame the objections of scientists who linked psychic research to nineteenth-century mysticism. He also appealed to a wider community of scholars, while at the

Apollo 14 astronaut Edgar D. Mitchell, who conducted scientific experiments on the moon, performed tests of his own during the 1971 voyage: He tried to send ESP symbols telepathically to psychics on earth. The results were inconclusive.

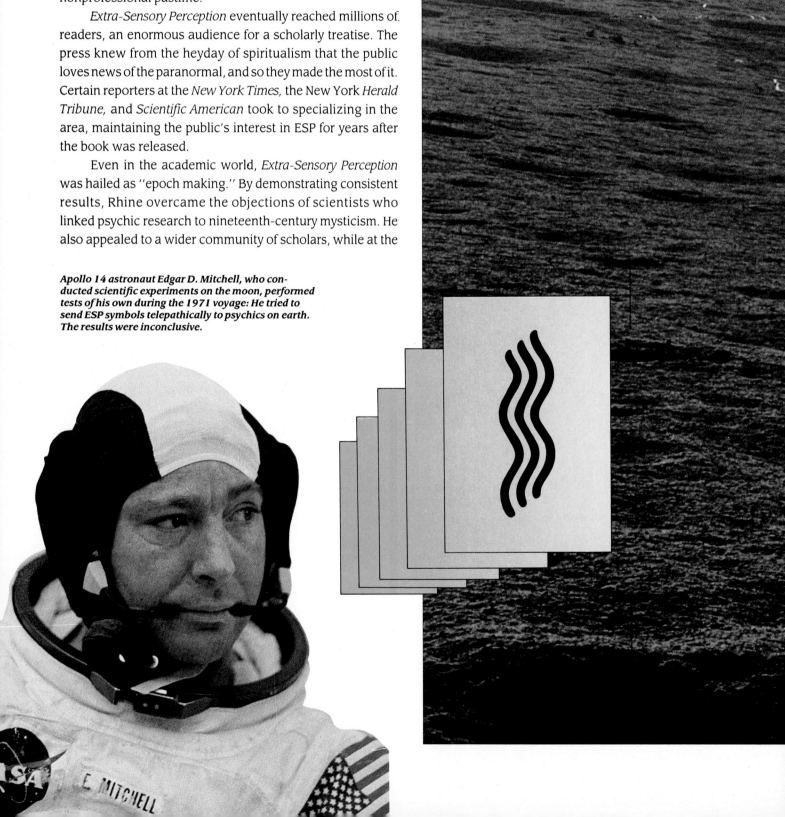

same time calming the psychic researchers who feared ESP would be inhibited by the strict conditions he imposed.

For all its acclaim, however, the book was highly controversial and stirred up criticism among psychologists and other traditional scientists. Some found fault with his statistics; not until 1937, when the American Institute of Mathematical Statistics declared his mathematics to be valid, were the statistical critics silenced. More serious were the attacks on some of Rhine's early procedures. Skeptics observed that a test in which a single unsupervised experimenter conducts the session and records the results—the very situation in which Pearce guessed his twenty-five out of twenty-five cards—has few safeguards against fraud or error. For example, cards that are hand shuffled, as in these early tests, will not yield a completely new and random arrangement each time. This allows subjects who remember the previous shuffle to improve their scores on each run-through. Furthermore, unconscious physical reactions of the experimenter—say, tilting the head every time a star comes up—can provide information to the subject, as was later shown in tests by British scientist S. G. Soal *(pages 110-111)*. To Rhine's credit, he soon realized these potential sources of error and tightened his procedures. He removed experimenters from the room containing subjects, added extra researchers to supervise tests and double-check results, and introduced a machine to shuffle cards. (His critics pointed out that Rhine's results were much less impressive after he instituted these controls.)

Probably the main criticism scientists had of Rhine's work was that it proved to be unrepeatable. In other areas of science, experimental results are considered questionable unless they can be reproduced by independent researchers. This unreproducibility of ESP experiments has remained a major stumbling block to widespread acceptance of parapsychology as a legitimate science—and even raises questions about ESP's very existence.

Partly as a result of the furor over Rhine's work, the Duke University administration carefully separated parapsychology from psychology and the other traditional sciences. But McDougall's response was more assured. With funds from Frances T. Bolton, an Ohio philanthropist, he established the country's first university parapsychology laboratory in a building near the Duke University campus and made Rhine its founding director. *Extra-Sensory Perception* also got a warm welcome from McDougall's old protégé Gardner Murphy, who had continued psychic research while building a reputation in traditional psychology at Columbia. Rhine sent graduate students to Murphy for advanced research, and New York became another stronghold of ESP testing. In 1937, Murphy helped Rhine found the *Journal of Parapsychology* for disseminating the latest developments in paranormal studies. New research centers at other universities cropped up frequently thereafter, and soon the press was predicting that parapsychology would be the science of the future.

Rhine's book also earned him an admirer among the century's intellectual pioneers—the eminent Swiss psychiatrist Carl Jung, who wrote to congratulate him and to offer some reassurance against the uphill battle Rhine would continue to face. "There are things," Jung said, "which are simply incomprehensible to the tough brains of our race and time. One simply risks being taken for crazy or insincere, and I have received so much of the other that I learned to be careful in keeping quiet." But now that he was launched, Rhine had no intention of keeping his work under wraps. Showing the sort of self-assurance that had kept him going in dark days, he wrote, "In the history of more than one branch of research, the stone which a hasty science rejected has sometimes become the cornerstone of its later structure."

For the most part, Rhine's focus remained the endless refinements of target guessing. Some of his young colleagues, impatient with card counting, wanted to rush into more exotic areas such as reincarnation and out-of-body experiences, but Rhine would have none of those — and may therefore have saved the infant discipline from deadly ridicule. Eventually the field would grow to encompass many of these other experiences, and the word psi would become the umbrella term for psychic abilities of every kind. But the main work to be done, as Rhine saw it, was to look for traces of ESP in all people, and as a rule he avoided self-professed psychic stars, reasoning

Psychiatrist and psi enthusiast Carl Jung followed Rhine's work closely, once writing to him about this household knife, which had mysteriously exploded in Jung's kitchen. No cause was ever found.

that if ESP were a natural human trait it could be found in the population at large.

Occasionally, Rhine took time out for other research, most notably in the field of ESP in animals, or anpsi, as parapsychologists are wont to call it. The idea that animals could have ESP was even more unusual than the thought of ESP in humans, but Rhine had practical reasons for wanting to study animals: They were easier to control and could be counted on not to cheat or exaggerate.

The Rhines had first investigated anpsi on their way down to Duke in 1927. They stopped in Richmond, Virginia, to investigate a horse named Lady Wonder that had achieved national attention for having what appeared to be psychic abilities. By nuzzling children's alphabet blocks to spell out words, Lady foretold events; one of her alleged predictions was the victory of boxer Jack Dempsey over Gene Tunney in 1927. The Rhines later returned to Richmond with McDougall to study Lady in depth and found that her performance diminished when her owner was not present and eventually deteriorated to chance levels—raising the distinct possibility that the horse had been receiving subtle signals. Thereafter, Rhine experimented variously with rats, pigeons, and cats. Declassified documents reveal that in the 1950s, Rhine ran a series of secret tests for the U.S. Army to see if German shepherds could be trained to detect land mines through ESP. The dogs did well, but Rhine thought they might have relied on their acute sense of smell rather than on ESP.

In 1969, ESP researchers achieved a measure of the official recognition they had long craved. The Parapsychological Association, formed twelve years before by Rhine and others in the field, was admitted to affiliate status in the American Association for the Advancement of Science (AAAS), the leading organization of U.S. scientists. If the hypothesis of ESP and other phenomena had not been finally proven, parapsychology could at least claim legitimacy as an area of scientific research. But it had scarcely gained its hard-won esteem when it suffered a setback. Unfortunately for Rhine, the reversal came as the result of fraud within his own ranks.

Nature's Sensory Spectrum

The term extrasensory perception implies unnatural, even supernatural, abilities. But research into the senses of some animals suggests that the line between sensory and extrasensory may be finer than previously imagined.

Animals have sense organs that react to stimuli humans cannot even detect. For example, some birds hear infrasound — noise in ultralow frequencies undiscernible to human ears. Many migrate for thousands of miles, using sensory navigational skills scientists have yet to explain. "Birds are not living in the same sensory world that we live in," explains Stephen T. Emlen, a professor at Cornell University and a leader in avian research. "They are hearing, seeing, and sensing a world expanded from ours."

Emlen's statement holds true for other creatures as well. Marine animals communicate underwater by sound beyond the limits of human hearing; schools of fish move and change direction simultaneously, presumably cued by signals. Flying bats are guided by their heightened sense of hearing; some distinguish between poisonous and nonpoisonous prey by using sensors on their mouths.

Some psychic researchers theorize that senses such as these may once have existed in humans, only to be submerged somehow in the evolutionary process. Perhaps, they say, people with apparent psychic powers are merely tapping into once-used but long-forgotten abilities.

Migratory birds, such as the trumpeter swans at right, can orient themselves visually by landmarks. Research shows that birds may also be guided by a sense of the earth's magnetic and gravitational fields.

A hungry bat advances on a toad; moments later, the bat will retreat, alerted by sensitive protrusions around its mouth that the quarry is poisonous. Bats navigate — and find food — by emitting ultrasonic squeaks that bounce off objects and are picked up by the animal's acute sense of hearing.

A school of silversides swerves as a unit to avoid an intruder. Marine biologists theorize that as one fish senses danger and begins to move away, it somehow sends an immediate signal to the rest of the school. The result is a simultaneous change in course.

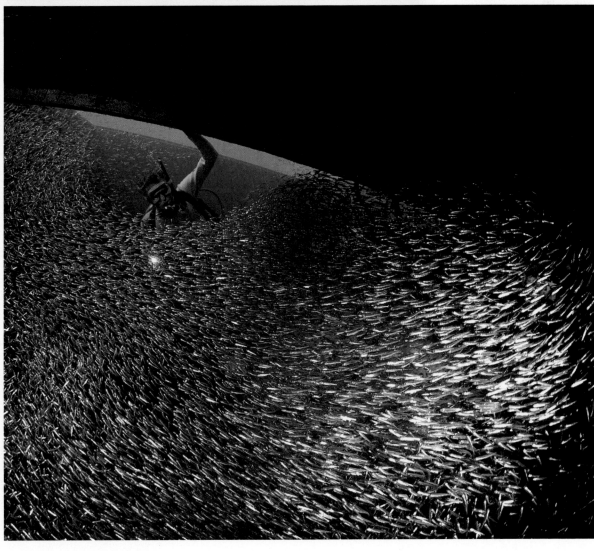

In 1973, Rhine appointed a young medical school graduate named Walter Jay Levy to succeed him as director of an institution called the Foundation for Research on the Nature of Man, which Rhine had established in 1962 with privately raised funds so that research in ESP would continue after he retired from the field. Rhine was in his seventies by this time and looking for an intellectual heir. Levy seemed a splendid choice, even though some colleagues thought him overly ambitious and prone to political machinations. For Rhine's purposes, the young scientist's virtues easily outstripped his faults. Brilliant and innovative, Levy had written numerous papers on experimental research. He was ingenious at designing experiments, and his subjects ranged through a staggering gamut from humans to chicken embryos. Levy was also remarkably energetic and single-minded. When he had an experiment under way, it was not uncommon for him to sleep in his lab to stay close to it. All in all, the usually crusty Rhine found his young protégé worthy of his faith and regard.

In 1974, Levy was experimenting on rats, implanting electrodes in the pleasure centers of their brains to see if they could give themselves a jolt of happiness by willing the electrodes to turn on. For a time he seemed to be getting positive results, but two of his fellow researchers, James Davis and James Kennedy, suspected that he was tampering with his

data. They decided to set a trap for him. In the early evening of June 11, they ran an extra set of cables from Levy's computer into a second computer in another room so that they could examine Levy's raw data as it was generated. Davis then hid in Levy's computer room and waited.

Sure enough, late that night, Davis saw Levy come in and force the computer to record a string of hits, while the raw data that were pouring into Kennedy's computer showed chance results. Davis and Kennedy informed Rhine, Rhine summoned Levy, Levy confessed, and Rhine fired him. The episode was disappointing on its own terms, but for Rhine it was doubly distressing because he had to make the painful sacrifice of publicizing the circumstances of Levy's departure so that others would not be misled by his research results.

If that was not enough, Rhine was publicly attacked in 1979 from other quarters for other reasons. The renowned physicist John A. Wheeler—who originated the theory of black holes—was a firm opponent of psi, and when he learned that a paper he was scheduled to deliver at an AAAS meeting in Houston would be followed by a discussion with parapsychologists, he hastily wrote two blistering indictments entitled "Drive the Pseudos out of the Workshop of Science" and "Where There's Smoke, There's Smoke."

Wheeler delivered these blasts as speeches at the AAAS

meeting. "Every science that is a science has hundreds of hard results," he said, "but search fails to turn up a single one in 'parapsychology.' " He then called for stripping the Parapsychological Association of its coveted affiliation, declaring that if "confidence men can be sent to jail" the AAAS should feel under no obligation to lend an "air of legitimacy" to psi. Later, in a panel discussion, he asserted that fifty years previously, while an assistant to McDougall, Rhine had skewed the results on a psychology experiment.

Rhine was recovering from a stroke when he heard of this accusation. He got a transcript of Wheeler's comments, saw that it was full of errors, and in a letter to the AAAS journal called Wheeler on them. Wheeler replied, retracting the accusation that Rhine had cheated—but standing fast on his opinion that psi was illegitimate science.

Retired California police official Pat Price astounded psi researchers during a 1974 remote-viewing test when he correctly described a sailing marina (left) — the destination of a car driven at random — twenty minutes before the driver decided to stop there. Price performed similar feats seven times in a series of nine tests, against odds calculated at 100,000 to one.

In effect, Rhine had the last word; when he died several months later, in 1980, his half-century of accomplishments outweighed the hostility of critics such as Wheeler. Parapsychology had spread over the globe during his lifetime, and he left a rich legacy of terminology and testing procedures. But the problems that dogged Rhine continue to plague psychic research: Psi effects seem fleeting at best, most experiments are irreproducible, errors and fraud abound despite tighter experimental procedures. The field has, however, acquired the patina of age. In the U.S. alone, parapsychology is researched and taught at an estimated 100 colleges and universities. It is also studied in a number of other countries, among them Great Britain, France, Germany, the Netherlands, India, Japan, and the Soviet Union. Moreover, the field is becoming sophisticated. Zener cards remained standard well into the 1960s, but high-technology equipment has largely replaced the tedious and error-prone manual testing. The majority of para-psychologists nowadays use computers to register test results directly, rather than ask researchers to keep hand-written records—which have proved susceptible to mistakes as well as to alteration. They also churn out ESP targets with special machines called Random Event Generators (REGs). These are useful because statisticians have found that it is simply impossible for humans to choose numbers or objects in a truly random way. When they are asked to choose a number between one and ten, for example, most people will pick seven. Those attempting to choose a series of numbers at random will avoid repeating the same one and will try to get an even distribution of different numbers—resulting, in the long run, in predictable, nonrandom patterns.

One of the first REGs, made to test for precognition, was built by German-born Dr. Helmut Schmidt while he was a

In a 1978 remote-viewing test, subject Hella Hammid sketched an unfamiliar airport tower (left) about three miles from her Menlo Park, California, location. She described the target as "a square tower with leaflike protrusions around it. . . . Something mechanical, something that needs to be visible from the sky . . . like . . . an airport tower."

physicist at Boeing Research Laboratories. The heart of his machine was a piece of radioactive strontium 90, an unstable element that emits electrons as it decays. This entirely random fallout drove four colored lights; subjects guessed which light would be lit next.

In one series on Schmidt's machine, subjects predicted correctly 26.7 percent of the time, more than the expected twenty-five percent that chance would decree. To the average layperson, so small an increment as 1.7 percent might not seem very impressive, but when maintained over long periods of testing it assumes a validity that social scientists refer to as "statistically significant." Thus, the equipment and the results that it produced led some mainstream scientists to take notice.

For subjects, too, the new machinery has brought a welcome change. It makes possible a variety of interesting targets, which help keep subjects more involved in experiments. In the mid-1980s, for example, researchers at the Psychophysical Research Laboratory, located in Princeton, New Jersey, developed a format somewhat like an arcade computer game to keep subjects from

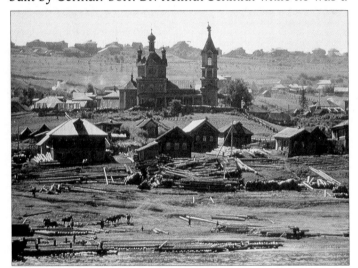

Given only longitude and latitude coordinates, Keith Harary sketched the Russian sawmill town of Kamenka (left) in a 1980 remote-viewing test. Drawings (below) revealed terrain and buildings and "beaten up wooden poles."

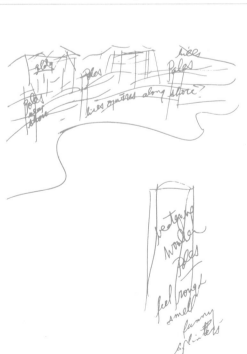

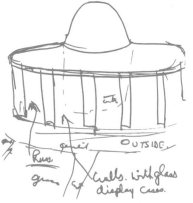

As a researcher gazed at the Louisiana Superdome (left) in 1976, a subject in California drew the sketches shown here and described "a large circular building with a white dome" resembling "a flying saucer in the middle of a city"—almost the exact words the researcher had spoken into his tape recorder moments before.

getting bored during extended sessions of testing.

A number of parapsychologists, having decided that there is already substantial evidence for the existence of psi, have moved on to explore the conditions that seem to enhance ESP performance. In the 1950s, Gertrude Schmeidler, an experimental psychologist at the City College of New York, pursued this so-called process-oriented research by examining the relation between personality traits and psychic ability. She tested more than 1,300 people for ESP. Before they were tested, all of the subjects were asked to indicate whether they believed in ESP. Schmeidler called those who believed the sheep, and she demonstrated that they scored significantly higher than those she called the goats, who did not believe—and who, interestingly, performed worse than chance. Schmeidler concluded that the goats were blocking their latent psychic abilities by unconsciously avoiding the assigned target.

Process-oriented research has also been used to try to counteract the decline effect. By moving from forced-choice targets—such as Zener cards—to free-response targets, some experimenters hoped they could approximate spontaneous ESP experiences more closely and involve subjects more

deeply in test procedures. The most celebrated example of a free-response experiment was conducted at Menlo Park, California, one afternoon in 1974. It began when Harold Puthoff, a physicist, seated himself in a car at the Stanford Research Institute (later renamed SRI International) with his boss, Dr. Bonnar Cox. Their plan was that they would drive aimlessly for thirty minutes. They had no idea where their journey would take them, nor did anyone else in the world—with the apparent exception of a man who was shut in an electrically shielded room on the second floor of SRI's engineering sciences building.

The man was Pat Price, retired police commissioner of Burbank, California. During his career in law enforcement, said Price, he had regularly used psychic powers to catch criminals. Now, he was about to put his alleged talents to a laboratory test. With Price was Russell Targ, a physicist. At 3:05, Targ turned on a tape recorder and started to explain that this experiment was being conducted to examine a psychic phenomenon called remote viewing. Targ told Price that when the two outbound investigators reached their destination, Price would be asked to describe what he saw there.

At that point, Price broke into the recording: "We don't have to wait till then," he said. "I can tell you right now where they will be. What I'm looking at is a little boat jetty or a little boat dock along the bay. . . . I see some motor launches, some little sailing ships. Sails all furled, some with their masts stepped, others are up. . . . Funny thing—this just flashed in . . . a definite feeling of Oriental architecture that seems to be fairly adjacent to where they are."

By the time Price finished his interruption it was 3:10; Cox and Puthoff still had another twenty minutes of aimless driving ahead of them. At 3:30 they pulled off the road and got out of the car. They were standing at the Redwood City Marina,

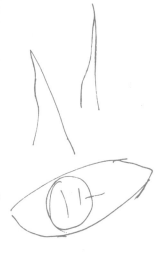

In 1984, Soviet psychic healer Djuna Davitashvili described, from 10,000 miles away, the carousel (above) a California researcher would randomly choose to visit hours later. Her sketch of "an animal's eye and pointy ears" (right) and vision of "a white divan" corresponded with seats on the children's ride.

63

A Meeting Foretold

When Miss J. K. *(below)* volunteered in 1958 to take part in Milan Ryzl's hypnotic ESP experiments the Prague accounting clerk—whose name was withheld for privacy—had never experienced ESP. But Ryzl believed that ESP could be taught and refined through hypnosis, and, by their second session, it appeared that J. K. might prove his theory true. Under Ryzl's tutelage—and a light trance—J. K. seemed able to predict future occurrences in the lives of her friends or relatives.

During one exercise, J. K. foresaw a meeting the following day between Ryzl and a friend he had not seen for some time. Ryzl decided to find out if predicted events could be averted. "When the meeting was predicted," he explained later, "I assumed that I would meet this person on a street, as was the case in earlier meetings. To avoid it, I decided to stay the whole next day at home." However, J. K.'s prediction was proved accurate: According to Ryzl, the friend appeared at his door for a visit.

What Dreams Are Made Of

Human beings have always been intrigued by their dreams. From the moment we awake, most of us struggle to recapture and understand the elusive images that flitted through our minds during the night. Scientists and psychologists, too, search for the meanings of dreams, but usually while addressing larger questions: When, precisely, do dreams occur? What causes them? What is their purpose? Might they even, as some parapsychologists maintain, serve as channels for psychic communication?

As long ago as the early 1900s, researchers began to make the connection between the state of dreaming and rapid eye movements, or REMs—short bursts of eye wiggling followed by a minute or two of rest—during certain periods of sleep. In the 1950s, the correlation between REM activity and dreaming was reinforced by studies in which electroencephalographs monitored the brain waves of sleeping volunteers. Researchers found that most sleepers progress through four stages of sleep, ranging from light slumber to deep sleep. About ninety minutes after falling asleep, this pattern is reversed.

While ascending through the sleep stages, the sleeper may be difficult to rouse, but the brain registers alertness. This is the REM stage *(above),* and here dreams take place. This pattern is repeated four to five times per night, with each dream period lasting for approximately ten minutes.

During all sleep stages, dream researchers monitor (above, from top) eye movements, muscle tone, and brain waves.

Less easy to uncover, however, has been the cause of dreams. One neurophysiological explanation is that dreaming is a side effect of concentrated nerve signals traveling within the brain; another view holds that during REM sleep the central nervous system is clearing itself of chemicals generated during the day. However, neither theory addresses the content of dreams. That task has usually fallen to psychologists.

Sigmund Freud felt that dreams express unconscious wishes and desires. Carl Jung viewed them as glimpses into the collective unconscious, filled with symbols that contain advice or guidance. Some scientists believe that dreams are a way for the mind to rid itself of excess information; still others consider dreams the means by which humans integrate new knowledge about their environment and rehearse responses to various situations. But no single theory has accounted for the full range of dream experiences, including those with alleged psychic content. Large-scale, systematic experiments have convinced a number of psychic investigators that telepathic exchange during dreams is not rare and does not require a special aptitude. Although thoughts or images may not always be transmitted whole from sender to dreamer, parts may be interwoven with the ongoing dream or appear in an analogous form.

Taking dream telepathy research one step further, Dr. Keith Hearne of Hull, England, is studying the lucid dream, in which the sleeper knows a dream is occurring. Hearne has developed a device that monitors the sleeper's breathing, and when the subject breathes in a prearranged pattern to indicate a dream has begun, the machine automatically telephones a sender. The sender then concentrates on delivering an image to the alerted dreamer.

Dream studies continue to be conducted, but dream researchers Montague Ullman and Stanley Krippner have already drawn some conclusions. "The psyche of man possesses a latent ESP capacity that is most likely to be deployed during sleep," they have written. "It took many hundreds of thousands of years before man learned to write his language. How much longer will it take before he learns to use his psi?"

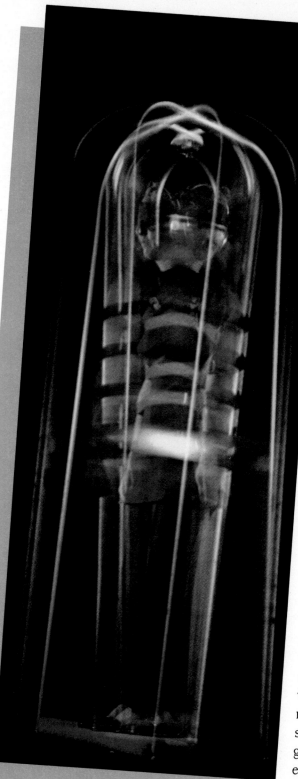

a harbor and boat dock some four miles from SRI. Small and medium-size sailboats and motorboats were bobbing lazily in the water; a modern, Oriental-looking restaurant stood nearby. From all indications, Price had not only envisioned the marina from a windowless room miles away; he had also correctly predicted that Puthoff and Cox would end up there, long before they had arrived.

The remote-viewing experiments of Targ and Puthoff continued at SRI International for more than a decade. The SRI team expanded remote-viewing attempts over incredible distances. Subjects in Menlo Park with varying degrees of apparent success tried to perceive targets at sites as distant as New York and San Andreas, Colombia. One subject in Detroit seemed to come close to identifying her sender's view of Rome International Airport. Another subject, a photographer by the name of Hella Hammid, was judged to have described correctly five out of nine target sites, a feat that beat odds of half a million to one. Following that success, she underwent a particularly severe test.

In July 1977, she was placed in a small submarine, towed two miles out into the Pacific Ocean off the California coast, and submerged. She knew that her telepathic "beacon"—who would go to the target she had to identify—would be located somewhere in the San Francisco Bay area, but that was all.

Despite some seasickness, Hammid was able to "see" the target; her beacon had climbed a large oak tree on a cliff overlooking Stanford University. While submerged, Hammid recorded the tree, the cliff, and the fact that her beacon was behaving in a very "unscientific fashion." Presumably, she picked up on his peculiar movements but could not discern that he was climbing a tree.

Although these remote-viewing experiments had reasonably tight experimental controls, critics have still found room for error or even fraud in Targ's and Puthoff's procedures. In some tests, for instance, subjects knew that ten viewing targets were selected one at a time, and they were told at the end of a session which targets had been visited. This would allow the subject to rule out previously chosen targets. Similarly, judges were supposed to choose hits or misses by matching transcripts of the subject's descriptions with actual targets. However, the transcripts apparently contained a number of clues—for instance, references to places visited the day before—which would cue the judges to the correct match. Some critics have even charged that Targ and Puthoff did not report many of their negative results, a charge the two scientists deny.

While such process-oriented research has been examining external influences on psychic abilities, other investigations have been exploring how internal changes can affect

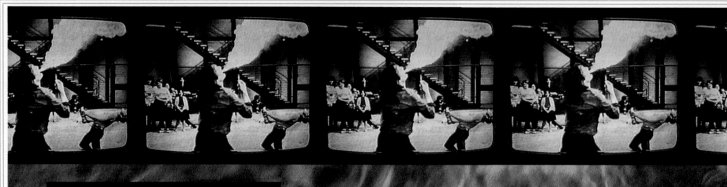

The Ganzfeld Cocoon

An intriguing area of psychic investigation today is *ganzfeld* (German for "whole field") research. Developed in 1971 by parapsychologist Charles Honorton, the ganzfeld environment is considered an analogue of the highly relaxed dream state, in which psychic powers are said to flourish.

The subject lies quietly in a darkened room, bathed in a dim red light. Halved table-tennis balls cover his eyes, and headphones fill his ears with the synthesized sounds of white noise. Alert and relaxed, but deprived of normal sensory stimulation, the subject turns inward, focusing on the images that come unchecked into his mind.

In one such experiment, in 1984, an ESP test subject outfitted for ganzfeld research relaxed in a room at the Psychophysical Research Laboratories in Princeton. Meanwhile, in another room, a sender concentrated on a photograph—flashed at intervals on a TV monitor of two fire-eaters *(top)*, intent on transmitting the picture telepathically to the subject. The ganzfeld subject described his thoughts as follows:

"This white noise, which ordinarily sounds like water, this time seems like flames . . . again hearing the rush of flames. I am reminded of a funeral pyre, I remember a picture of Gandhi's body being burned, but so far the fire images haven't been unpleasant. My images of flames didn't really include the feeling of heat. Red color, red-orange color together."

psi. This area of experimentation, called Altered States Research (ASR), tests the notion that when we loosen our grip on everyday reality we open ourselves up to a world of communication deep within our minds.

Since the Oracle at Delphi in ancient Greece, psychics have claimed to tap powers of clairvoyance and precognition by going into trances. In the eighteenth century, the Austrian physician and mystic Anton Mesmer developed the techniques of hypnosis to try to produce a similar state in his subjects. Rhine conducted some unfruitful experiments with hypnosis but discontinued them when he learned that his students were hypnotizing each other for fun in their rooms.

In the early 1960s, however, the Czech biochemist Milan Ryzl used hypnosis to make parapsychology history. Ryzl hypnotized a subject named Pavel Stepanek into believing in his psychic powers, and Stepanek emerged as an astoundingly high scorer at card guessing, sometimes against odds of 500,000 to one. Stepanek went on to perform impressively in all sorts of conditions over a decade. One parapsychologist described this as "the longest period on record of a successful demonstration of ESP by a subject in laboratory tests." Skeptics, however, have pointed out that Stepanek was permitted to handle the card packages during the experiments, thus raising the possibility of some sort of cheating.

Besides using hypnosis, researchers have sought to induce altered states through drugs, meditation, biofeedback, and a technique called ganzfeld, a German term meaning, roughly, "total field." In the ganzfeld setting, subjects are isolated from the external environment by having opaque hemispheres—halved table-tennis balls—put over their eyes and white noise played to them through earphones. By letting their minds wander, subjects try to respond to information projected mentally by an isolated sender *(left)*.

Sleep is a naturally altered state, and there is abundant anecdotal evidence that it enhances psychic ability. Louisa Rhine collected data on 100,000 spontaneous psi occurrences over twenty years; her analysis showed that sixty-five percent of them occurred in dreams. In one, a woman in North Wales saw, on March 4, 1871, an image of her distant son in ill health.

Three Theories of ESP

Parapsychologists face two basic challenges: proving that psychic powers exist and, if so, explaining how they work. Most psi researchers have quite logically devoted themselves to the first problem. However, the absence of a coherent theory of ESP has cast doubt on the entire field. Critics point out that psychic powers are so unlikely from a scientific point of view that any other explanation for positive experimental results, including fraud, must be considered first.

Indeed, telepathy, clairvoyance, and precognition seem to contradict the elementary physical laws that govern our lives. How can information travel from person to person, or from event to person, without following known sensory channels? Standard physics dictates that no signals of any kind can travel faster than the speed of light and that as they travel, they lose strength. How then can parapsychologists account rationally for precognition, in which information from an event is said to reach the subject before the event occurs? How can they explain the way in which a telepathic message allegedly arrives at its target undiminished by intervening distances?

Some psychic researchers have responded to these questions with theories, or at least interpretations of theories, suggesting that psychic effects may not be incompatible with modern scientific thought. Such researchers speculate that some physical descriptions of the universe might serve as models, or metaphors, for the way psychic phenomena behave. Among these models are electromagnetism, multidimensional geometry, and quantum mechanics, illustrated on the next three pages.

VISIBLE LIGHT

X RAY

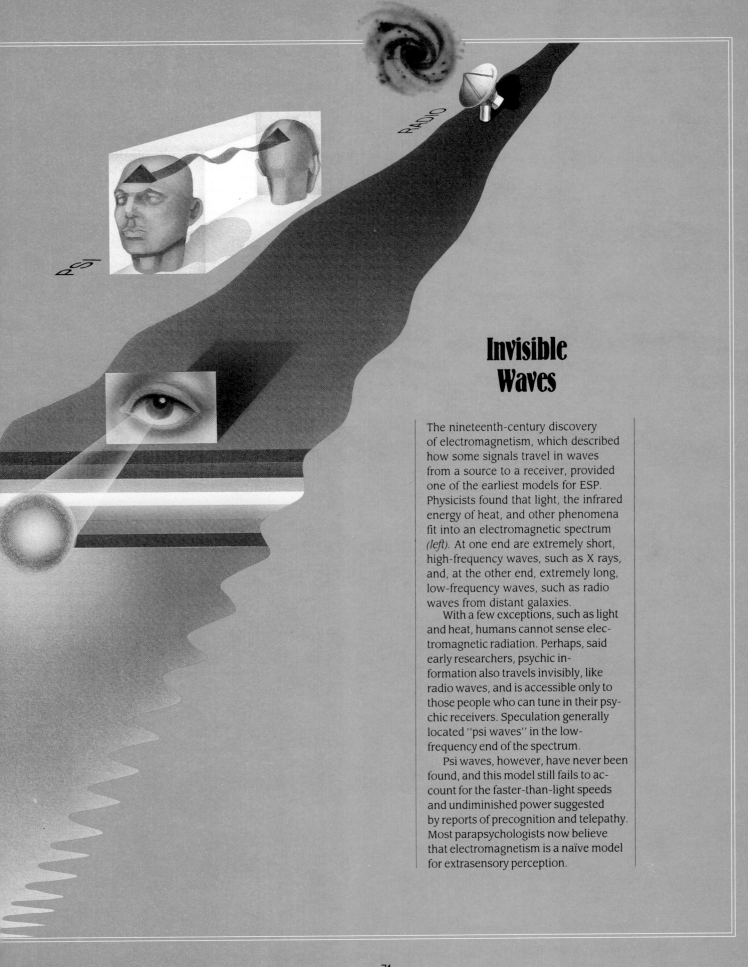

RADIO

PSI

Invisible
Waves

The nineteenth-century discovery
of electromagnetism, which described
how some signals travel in waves
from a source to a receiver, provided
one of the earliest models for ESP.
Physicists found that light, the infrared
energy of heat, and other phenomena
fit into an electromagnetic spectrum
(left). At one end are extremely short,
high-frequency waves, such as X rays,
and, at the other end, extremely long,
low-frequency waves, such as radio
waves from distant galaxies.

With a few exceptions, such as light
and heat, humans cannot sense electromagnetic radiation. Perhaps, said
early researchers, psychic information also travels invisibly, like
radio waves, and is accessible only to
those people who can tune in their psychic receivers. Speculation generally
located "psi waves" in the low-
frequency end of the spectrum.

Psi waves, however, have never been
found, and this model still fails to account for the faster-than-light speeds
and undiminished power suggested
by reports of precognition and telepathy.
Most parapsychologists now believe
that electromagnetism is a naïve model
for extrasensory perception.

The Psi
Dimension

Another, more recent model for supposed psychic effects places them in a dimension outside of — but interacting with — the four dimensions of space and time we can perceive. These are illustrated symbolically here: If a line, with only the single dimension of height, moves through space, its shape over time is a plane — a shape in the two dimensions of height and width. The plane, moved through space and time to gain depth, will form the outlines of a three-dimensional cube as it travels.

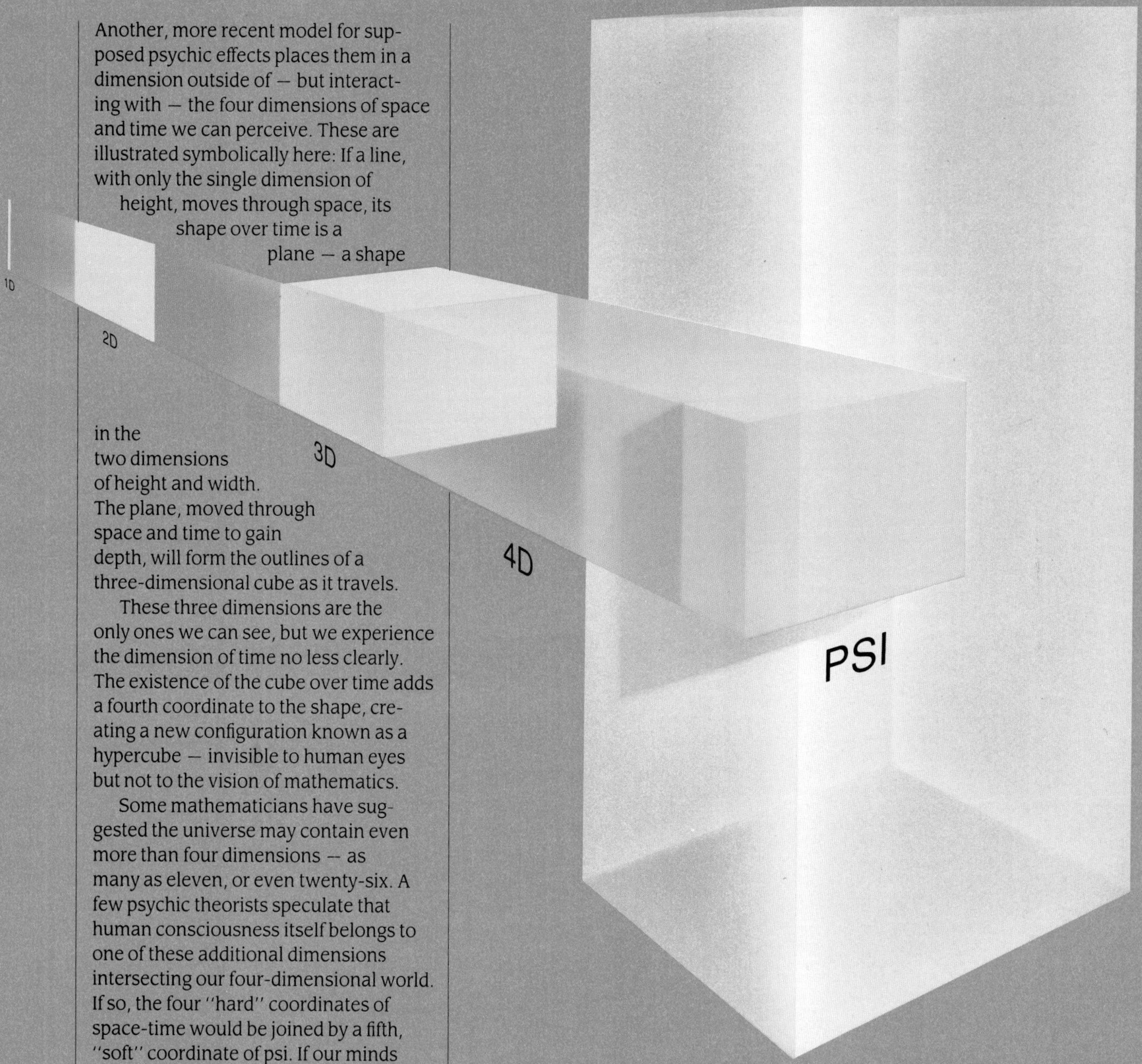

These three dimensions are the only ones we can see, but we experience the dimension of time no less clearly. The existence of the cube over time adds a fourth coordinate to the shape, creating a new configuration known as a hypercube — invisible to human eyes but not to the vision of mathematics.

Some mathematicians have suggested the universe may contain even more than four dimensions — as many as eleven, or even twenty-six. A few psychic theorists speculate that human consciousness itself belongs to one of these additional dimensions intersecting our four-dimensional world. If so, the four "hard" coordinates of space-time would be joined by a fifth, "soft" coordinate of psi. If our minds could somehow tap into this extra dimension, the way information travels outside of the natural laws we presently know might be explained. However, with no physical evidence to support extra dimensions, the idea of a consciousness plane remains nothing more than fascinating speculation.

1D

2D

3D

4D

PSI

A Quantum Connection

One of the most popular current metaphors for psychic communication relies on the paradoxical world view of quantum mechanics. This science describes the behavior of matter at the subatomic level, where basic units are neither particles nor waves but act like both, and where matter cannot even be said definitely to exist. Rather, it has a "tendency to exist," expressed as a mathematical probability.

The micro world of subatomic behavior follows different rules from the macro world we know. A famous example of this is the paradox illustrated above. In this thought experiment, two particles — say, an electron and its antimatter equivalent, a positron — collide, annihilating each other and creating two photons, which speed off in different directions. By the strange laws of quantum mechanics, photon A does not possess properties such as spin or velocity until it is noted by an observer; the very act of measurement is said to "collapse its wave function" and assign it values at random. At the moment that observers do measure photon A, causing it to acquire a certain spin, photon B will acquire the opposite spin, no matter how far away it is, and despite having no connection with the first particle. Photon B somehow seems to "know" instantaneously what photon A is doing.

This occurrence, confirmed in physical experiments, suggests that the universe is connected in some hidden way, perhaps at a hypothetical sub-quantum level that includes our consciousness. If so, then clairvoyance, which supposedly enables a psychic to know instantly of an airplane crash miles away, may become plausible.

She later learned that he had died in Africa that same evening. The most famous series of attempts to track dream telepathy was conducted in 1965 by Drs. Montague Ullman and Stanley Krippner at their laboratory for dream research at Maimonides Medical Center in Brooklyn, New York. In this experiment, after a receiver had gone to sleep in one room, a sender in another room concentrated on a picture chosen randomly from a large selection at the lab.

Dreams are accompanied by Rapid Eye Movements (REMs). Sleeping receivers at Maimonides were connected to electroencephalographs to monitor their brain waves for REMs that would show when their dreams began. Receivers would be wakened in mid-dream to record what they had seen while dreaming.

The Maimonides team took extraordinary measures against cheating, intentional and otherwise. Rooms were soundproofed; pictures were sealed and signed across their seals, and signatures were covered with tape. The images the dreamers described were compared with the senders' pictures by independent judges to see if there were correspondences.

The results were often surprisingly on target. One sender was given a picture of George Bellows's *Dempsey and Firpo,* a dramatic painting of a prize fight in Madison Square Garden. The dreamer reported the following: "Something about posts. Just posts standing up from the ground and nothing else. There is some kind of feeling of movement. . . . Ah. Something about Madison Square Garden and a boxing fight."

Another subject demonstrated what some psychic researchers have interpreted as precognitive dreaming. She dreamed she saw a co-worker looking at the front page of the New York *Daily News* and seeing a collapsed building. He was not, in fact, doing any such thing at the time. But two weeks later, the Broadway Central Hotel caved in, and hundreds of thousands of New Yorkers saw its picture on the front page.

With these and other experiments, parapsychologists have attempted to follow the rest of the world into the age of science. They have kept their eyes on new scientific developments, tools, and methods. But their field still struggles for broad acceptance among mainstream scientists and psychologists. As one critic, psychologist David Mark, said: "Parascience has so far failed to produce a single repeatable finding and, until it does, will continue to be viewed as an incoherent collection of belief systems steeped in fantasy, illusion, and error."

To be sure, new developments in other sciences have occasionally led to a more open view of psi research. Theoretical physicists, for example, have proposed theories of the universe that allow for concepts such as time travel—making claims for psi seem almost conservative by comparison. And through the study of quantum mechanics—which deals with events within atoms—some physicists have concluded that reality must be defined as a relation between our minds and the things we observe, rather than as some objective, outside entity. A number of parapsychologists have tried to adapt these theories as explanations of psi phenomena *(page 70).*

An even more favorable development has been the emergence of so-called anomalistic psychology. In recent years psychologists have admitted the existence of what they call puzzles in psychology—repeatedly observed phenomena, such as apparently precognitive dreams, that cannot be fully explained with current knowledge. Although anomalistic psychologists do not attribute parapsychological answers to such puzzles, they do not dismiss them and are more open to examining the evidence for alternative explanations.

For all that, parapsychologists themselves are becoming more patient with traditional explanations and are no longer wedded to paranormal explanations for all mysterious phenomena. Indeed, the Parapsychological Association holds that the very existence of psi is still a hypothesis and not a validated fact. The association also states that "A commitment to the study of psi phenomena does not require assuming the reality of 'non-ordinary' factors or processes."

It is still too early to determine whether the uncertainties and unanswered questions that surround psi are symptoms of parapsychology's growing pains or indications that its goals will remain forever beyond human reach. But laboratory experimentation notwithstanding, the psychic world has been embraced by millions of ordinary people.

Mystic Powers of the Shamans

While claims of psychic powers are viewed by many today with a healthy dose of skepticism, some cultures accept contact with supernatural forces without question. Since earliest times, tribal societies have honored individuals believed to possess the ability to communicate with deities and spirits. Variously called seers, healers, or medicine men—but most widely known today as shamans—they are called upon to cure physical or emotional illness, secure food during times of famine, help find misplaced or stolen objects, predict the future, control the weather, retrieve the departing souls of the sick, and guide those of the dead.

Shamans usually try to contact the spirit world while in a trance. To reach this altered state of consciousness, they employ methods not unlike those used in some modern parapsychology experiments. They may meditate quietly or concentrate on the rhythmic sounds of drumming, singing, or dancing; they may fast or use hallucinogenic drugs. Once the mind and body have surrendered to the trance, the shaman is free to visit—often, it is said, through magical flight— the spirit world. There the shaman receives a message that may come in the form of a magic song, prayer, or ritual to be performed; it may also be an illuminating vision about the nature of life. On rare occasions, shamans have sought to describe, through words and pictures, some of the often ineffable messages they received during psychic odysseys to the spirit world. Examples from three tribal cultures—the Iglulik Eskimos, Oglala Sioux Indians, and Huichol Indians of Mexico— are shown on the following six pages.

The Spirits of Anarqâq

When the Danish explorer Knud Rasmussen arrived in arctic North America in 1921 to study the Iglulik Eskimos, he found a culture that revolved almost entirely around a multitude of unseen beings — spirits that inhabited every person, animal, and object, and unspecified spirits that were held responsible for seemingly inexplicable events such as illness and foul weather. With the aid of an Eskimo shaman named Anarqâq *(left)*, who recalled from his visions the beings shown here and painstakingly set them down on paper, Rasmussen learned that certain spirits were kind and helpful, others aggressive and malevo-lent, and some truly evil. Although the entire community worked to keep the bad spirits at bay by practicing prescribed rituals and taboos, only shamans were successful in banishing them completely.

As a shaman, Anarqâq was aided by so-called helping spirits. These were said to present themselves by invading a shaman's body or simply calling his name: When he answered, their power became his. Many kind spirits first appeared as monsters or ferocious animals that had to be conquered or subdued. But once helping spirits were won over, they remained steadfast, loyal, and readily available to the shaman.

Eskimo shaman Anarqâq

Anarqâq held that the spirit Igtuk was responsible for booming noises that were occasionally heard coming from the arctic mountains. As the shaman saw him, Igtuk had just one huge eye, which was set into his body at the same level as his arms. His mouth opened wide to disclose a dark abyss, and his chin was covered with a thick tuft of hair.

Soon after Anarqâq's parents died, he said, a melancholy spirit known as Issitôq, or Giant Eye, appeared. "You must not be afraid of me," the spirit entreated, "for I, too, struggle with sad thoughts. Therefore will I go with you and be your helping spirit." Issitôq, who had short, bristly hair, exceptionally long arms, and a vertical mouth with one long tooth and two short ones, helped Anarqâq find people who had broken the tribe's taboos.

In a vision that appeared to Anarqâq one spring day, a female spirit named Qungiaruvlik tried to steal a child by concealing it in her parka (above). Before she could accomplish the deed, however, two well-armed helping spirits came to the rescue and killed the kidnapper.

Kigutilik, one of many spirits that Anarqâq claimed to have encountered during hunting expeditions, was a monstrous being as big as a bear. With a mighty roar, Kigutilik arose from an opening in the ice as the shaman was hunting seal. Anarqâq was so frightened that he fled home without securing the spirit as helper.

Anarqâq confronted this rotund spirit, called Nârtôq, one day while hunting caribou. Nârtôq rushed at Anarqâq as if to attack him, but when the shaman prepared to defend himself, the spirit vanished. Later, Nârtôq reappeared and explained that if Anarqâq would learn to control his short temper, Nârtôq would become his helping spirit.

Led by two guides with flaming spears, Black Elk ascends on a cloud to visit the spirits. "I could see my mother and my father yonder," he recalled, "and I felt sorry to be leaving them."

As Black Elk was presented to the six Grandfathers—the spirits of the East, West, North, South, Earth, and Sky—he "shook all over with fear, for these were not old men, but the Powers of the World."

Black Elk's Great Vision

Black Elk prays to the spirits.

During his lifetime, Black Elk, an Oglala Sioux Indian chief and medicine man, had several visions that helped him guide his people through misfortunes. But his first journey to the spirit world occurred when Black Elk was a young boy. In 1931, the aged Black Elk recalled this vision for poet John G. Neihardt; Black Elk's boyhood friend, Standing Bear, illustrated the story with these drawings.

For a number of years spirit voices had called out and sung to Black Elk, he related, and when he reached the age of nine, the voices said: "It is time." With that, Black Elk suddenly fell ill and lay near death for twelve days; during this time, the great vision occurred.

Two spirits came down from the sky to fetch the boy from his home, he said, and with them Black Elk ascended to "a world of cloud . . . a great white plain with snowy hills and mountains." There, in a tepee adorned with a rainbow at its entrance, Black Elk met the six Grandfathers, the most powerful spirits of the world.

"They looked older than men can ever be," he said, "old like hills, like stars."

The Grandfathers taught Black Elk about the spiritual values of life and presented him with symbols of their powers: a cup of water and a sacred bow that make life or destroy it; the healing herb and cleansing sacred wind; the peace pipe and herb of understanding; the hoop of the world, symbolizing the universe; the flowering stick, symbol of the tree of life.

Then Black Elk was led to the center of the earth, where he was shown "the goodness and the beauty and the strangeness of the greening earth . . . the spirit shapes of things as they should be." His tutelage complete, Black Elk was dismissed by the oldest Grandfather, who told him: "Go back with power to the place from whence you came." Black Elk returned to his village; his illness was cured. But he had changed forever. The lightheartedness of boyhood had been transformed into the maturity of one who speaks with the knowledge of the ages.

From the center of the hoop of the world, Black Elk surveys each quadrant of the universe and the objects that symbolize its powers.

Demonstrating his newly acquired abilities, Black Elk uses a lightning-tipped sacred spear to turn the spirit of drought into a harmless turtle.

At the end of his vision, Black Elk views from the center of the earth "the shape of all shapes as they must live together like one being."

The Powers of Peyote

To Ulu Temay (right) and the other shamans of Mexico's Huichol Indians, a dreamless sleep is far worse than no sleep at all. For it is through dreams and visions that shamans receive messages from the gods. Their dreams may forecast future events, remind the shaman of obligations that he needs to fulfill or rituals that he should perform, reveal whether someone has offended the spirits, and suggest means for atonement.

But while dreams tell what must be accomplished, the Huichol shaman's actual powers are shown to him through peyote visions — kaleidoscopic images that appear after the shaman eats the hallucinogenic buttons, or tops, of the peyote cactus. Through the vision, the shaman leaves reality and enters an inner world where spirits share the secrets of their omnipotence and teach the shaman how to use and expand his powers.

While he eats these peyote buttons, the shaman may hold a brightly colored disk he has reproduced from one seen in earlier dreams. Such dream disks remind the shaman of a promise that he made to the gods during a previous vision; to fulfill his obligation, the shaman makes an offering of the disk.

The colored disks are also considered rewards from the gods for keeping a vow or a bargain and are thought to hold the essence — and thus the power — of the gods. In addition to colored disks, the shaman creates a tool of power by attaching bird feathers to arrows. Birds are thought to be messengers of the deities, and the feathered wands — when used together with the disks — create a channel for delivering messages to and from the gods.

The tools, kept in a woven basket such as the one held by Ulu Temay, are used in almost all shamanic rituals. They appear in the peyote vision described by the shaman and illustrated below, and in the vision of the rain-making ceremony shown on the opposite page.

Ulu Temay and shaman's tools

This yarn painting vividly recreates a peyote vision experienced by Ulu Temay. As the shaman explained: "The nealika [colored disk, center] promised me the healing energy of the sun, and the rain-making powers of the Rain Mothers. The sun and rain offered me the feathered wands. The deer spirits offered me their knowledge about how to use my powers with wisdom and precaution, and the eagle offered me his power to see all. The snakes are the voice of Grandfather Fire, who is the wisest and most powerful of all shamans. He spoke to me through the rattles on the snakes, and told me they will become my allies and make me strong against those who wish to do me harm."

In his rain-making ceremony, Ulu Temay uses feathered wands to contact the Rain Mothers. The Rain Mothers, he said, "live in the sea as serpents, and give birth to the Rain Child [bottom right], who turns into a serpent and guides my prayers up to the clouds. When it rains, baby serpents fall to the ground who are children of the Rain Mothers. The coiled serpent in the middle is the Earth Mother, who communicates with the serpents in the sea and sky, and thanks them for the nourishment they send. The people thank me, the shaman, for making the gods happy through my ceremony, and convincing the Rain Mothers to allow it to rain."

CHAPTER 3

The World of the Psychic

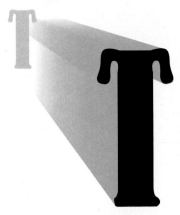

The room was all white except for dark brown wainscoting around its bottom half. A strong, astringent smell hung in the air, an odor that meant hospital to the small boy strapped onto the hard white table. Two-year-old Ingo Swann was about to undergo what the grownups called a tonsillectomy. He understood that the operation was necessary to make his throat stop hurting, but he also understood that he was afraid. Struggling against the restraining straps and caterwauling with all his might, he resisted the nurse's effort to cover his face with a dark mask. She retreated, only to return with a half-filled balloon.

"I bet you can't blow this up further," she teased. The air in the balloon smelled funny, but young Ingo took up the challenge. In moments, the room's bright lights began to fade and dim. Then—Ingo Swann would write long afterward—a strange thing happened. The white walls turned emerald, and the dark wainscoting took on an iridescent glow. Ingo felt himself hovering about three feet above his own body, secure in the shadows above the glare of the table, watching the surgery in progress. He gazed down at the doctor and the nurse and his mother, who had been allowed into the operating room to help calm him. He watched the scalpel slip and nick the back of his own tongue, and he heard the doctor curse in response. He watched the nurse put two small, brown objects—presumably his tonsils—into a bottle and stow them behind some rolls of tissue on a table against the wall.

Some time later, when Ingo came out from under the ether, he demanded to be given his tonsils.

"Now, now," the nurse said to the little boy, "We have already thrown those dirty things away."

"No you didn't," the child snapped, pointing toward the rolls of paper. "You put them behind those over there."

The doctor, the nurse, and his mother exchanged alarmed glances. Nobody spoke. The nurse had done exactly as Ingo said: The tonsils were in the bottle behind the rolls of paper on the table. The grownups could not understand how he could know—and he could not understand why he should not know. He often had the sensation of seeming to leave his own body and watching from a distance what was happening around it. But he had not yet learned that the experience, although known to psychics by a number of names—out-of-body experiences and astral travel among them—was not in the ken of most people.

Swann would grow up to become a noted psychic artist, his canvases filled with auric light he presumably saw emanating from the life he painted. For a time, discouraged by the cultural mind-set that viewed his claimed psychic powers as impossible, he stopped cultivating them. He eventually renewed an active interest, however, prompted partly by plants and animals. He noticed that he seemed to communicate telepathically with his pet chinchilla, which would exhibit great distress if Swann merely thought of putting it into its cage for the night. In addition, he felt he was able to receive mental signals from a bedraggled *Dracaena massangeana*—a common house plant. For example, Swann believed he could pick up on the plant's "mental" complaints of being watered too much or of lacking proper minerals in its soil.

Concluding to his own satisfaction that something noteworthy was going on, he submitted to testing by some of parapsychology's leading researchers. The results were often extraordinary. At the American Society for Psychical Research, for instance, he purportedly proved adept at remote viewing *(opposite)*, and in experiments with Dr.

Gertrude R. Schmeidler of the City University of New York, he demonstrated apparent psychokinesis—the ability to alter the physical environment, such as changing the air temperature inside sealed vacuum bottles, through mind power alone.

Still, his frustrations persisted. Although Swann greatly admired the work of Schmeidler and never abandoned psychic experimentation, he found much of it disillusioning. He concluded that science was too often wanting imagination and strictured by its own rationalist traditions, and that it was not yet up to the intricate task of exploring the world of the psychic. In the main, Swann said, researchers had "only succeeded in grinding the diamond into a dust pile while trying to capture the sparkle."

Yet, even as Swann wrote those words in a memoir published in 1975, the psychic world was exploding from the confines of the laboratory, where it had migrated from séance rooms and side shows only a few decades before. Blending with the neomysticism and antimaterialism of the 1960s and the self-realization movement of the 1970s, a pursuit of things psychic had at last infiltrated the mainstream of twentieth-century culture. Psychic powers were part of a loose amalgam that, in the years after Swann described his experiences, came under the general title the New Age. It was an age in which old definitions were expanded and blurred. Telepathy, clairvoyance, precognition, and retrocognition were all part of the New Age paraphernalia, but these aspects by no means circumscribed the movement. Whatever its tools, its goals were so-called higher consciousness, enlightened awareness.

New groups and movements arose to help psi enthusiasts escape the mundane world in ways ranging from simple meditation to astral voyaging and pagan rituals. Some aspirants to enlightenment flocked to so-called channelers, people who transmit purported sublime truths from spirits long dead. Others looked to psychic advisers to counsel them on their present lives, predict their futures, or even regress them through past existences.

Ingo Swann, who apparently possessed psi talents that most New Agers could merely aspire to, had little patience with the movement's mystical trappings. Believing the psychic impulse was of a piece with the creative urge in the human psyche and was in no way paranormal, he thought weird mysticism as great a trap as smug rationalism to those seeking a wider awareness of the universe. "Granted many individuals, their synapses misfiring or their alleged karma catching up with them, do sometimes go bonkers and create confusion among their fellow men," Swann wrote. "But, even so, this is no sign that all people whose imagination and consciousness wander beyond the immediate barriers of ideas of consciousness are bonkers."

Many detractors were less restrained in their contempt for New Age doings. Most traditional religionists warned against the psychic boom as idolatry. ESP skeptics insisted that years of scientific research had produced, at best, only the flimsiest evidence that psychic phenomena existed in any form. The ubiquitous New Agers, however, believed otherwise. No longer the province of academics on the one hand or the lunatic fringe on the other, the world of the psychic had become respectable, even fashionable in a way. And it was quite densely populated.

While the New Age was spawned partially by broad cul-

tural trends that directly preceded it, it was not without its individual progenitors. In particular, it owed a debt to two recent giants of psychism: Eileen Garrett and Edgar Cayce. They operated quite differently, but each seemed able—while unconscious—to gain access to information not available to the waking mind. Garrett functioned mostly as a medium—a conduit for spirits of the dead. Cayce was renowned as a psychic healer and a prophet. Firm conclusions about the nature of their apparent powers eluded both of these two people, though others theorized that clairvoyance, or telepathy, or both, figured in their work.

Garrett was born Eileen Jeanette Vancho in mist-shrouded County Meath in Ireland. She spent her childhood near the mystical Hill of Tara, a fey countryside where, she said later, "the 'little people' were universally accepted as an everyday part of normal existence." This myth-laden landscape was one of two factors she credited for the possible origin of her psychic gifts. The other was what she called "the almost equally universal acceptance of death as an intimate element of the daily round." She granted the possibility that the dead could communicate with the living and was fairly comfortable serving as a vehicle for the dialogue.

Certainly, death was an intimate specter in Garrett's personal life. Both her parents committed suicide while she was still an infant; one of her three husbands was killed in World War I, and only one of her four children survived into adulthood. But for all the death surrounding her, Garrett was anything but morbid.

"She hated to be deprived of any experience within her grasp—or even slightly beyond it," Garrett's daughter, Eileen Coley, has said. "She was such an entertaining personality—interested in so many things, so many people. If I could be fascinated by waking up at 7 A.M. to exchange funny stories with her, you can imagine what sort of person she was. A lot of people likened her to Auntie Mame." Indeed, according to Coley, novelist Patrick Dennis knew Garrett and used her as a prototype for his zany, globe-trotting heroine in *Auntie Mame.* It was Garrett's sheer force of personality, at least as much as

The Vision of Ingo Swann

Remote viewing—seeing beyond the range of physical vision—is one of several psychic talents attributed to Ingo Swann. To test his abilities, the American Society for Psychical Research devised an experiment in 1972. Pictures or objects were placed on a suspended platform; seated below it, pad and pencil in hand, Swann tried to see the images and then draw them while electrodes measured his brain's electrical activity *(above)*.

The substantially accurate sketches shown here, detailing shapes and colors of two abstract pictures on the platform, were among his successes. Swann believed he saw the objects by traveling out of his body, floating upward to where the pictures lay. Other possibilities considered by ASPR researchers are clairvoyance—having a vision of the pictures—or telepathy, reading the mind of someone who knew the platform's contents.

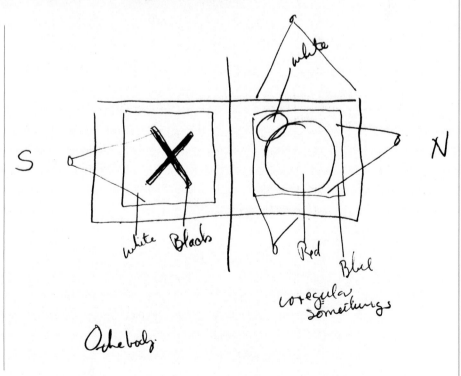

her alleged psychic gifts, that made such an impact on the many people she influenced.

Garrett left her native Ireland as a young woman and lived in London and the south of France before settling down in New York, becoming an American citizen, and undertaking a successful career in publishing. This was a reasonable enough direction for her life to take. From her youth, she had been something of a pet among the British literati, and her friends and acquaintances included D. H. Lawrence, Wil-

A pensive youth (above) and a dramatic flower appear to be surrounded by auras in these oil paintings by the widely tested psychic Ingo Swann.

liam Butler Yeats, George Bernard Shaw, Thomas Mann, Aldous Huxley, Robert Graves, and H. G. Wells.

In 1951, Garrett founded the Parapsychology Foundation, which supported scholarly and scientific research. The venture was funded mostly by the wealthy Ohio philanthropist Frances T. Bolton, who admired Garrett and was fascinated by paranormal phenomena. Over the years, other adherents of the medium also contributed, and Garrett volunteered money of her own. Through the organization, she funded expeditions to many parts of the world, spreading her passion to define and explain psychic powers. According to some of her friends, she was generous to a fault. Psychic researcher and anthropologist Eric J. Dingwall, who knew Garrett for almost half a century, sometimes despaired of her propensity for handing out money to almost any alleged researcher who asked for it. "It was but rarely that I succeeded in persuading her to refuse a grant to some patent swindler," Dingwall said. " 'You never know,' she used to say, 'there might be something and we mustn't miss it, must we?' "

Garrett's fascination with the mysterious and arcane seemed inbred and inexhaustible. She took an interest in voodoo, which she studied in Haiti and Jamaica. As a young woman Garrett even investigated the practice of devil worship, though more in a spirit of curiosity than commitment. She also submitted herself to the scrutiny of psychiatrists, psychologists, and neurologists, as well as to J. B. Rhine and other serious parapsychologists.

One famous experiment in 1931 tested Garrett's supposed ability to leave her body while in a trance and report on distant scenes she saw in her astral state. In a New York apartment, a psychiatrist and a secretary looked on while the medium tried to see into a doctor's office in Reykjavik, Iceland. In preparation for the experiment, the doctor had placed a number of items on an office table. Garrett was supposed to describe them. While in a trance, she did so, and then went on to repeat verbatim a passage from a book the physician was reading while the test took place. In addition, she reported that the doctor's head was bandaged. The doctor confirmed later that she had identified the objects correctly, quoted the book accurately, and, because of a slight accident that happened just before the experiment, his head had indeed been bandaged. He also reported sensing Garrett's presence in his office during the test.

Along with participating in experiments, Garrett tried to advance research by traveling widely to lecture on psychic phenomena—to Switzerland, Spain, the Scandinavian countries, Austria, Germany, Italy, Greece, India, Japan, and parts of South America. In the course of her travels, she would, if asked, conduct séances. But these meetings were not public events. Rather, they consisted of only small groups, often of only one or two friends.

As a medium, Garrett purportedly worked with several spirit guides, or controls, who identified themselves as long-dead individuals. Chief among the controls was an Oriental personage called Uvani. Seeming to act as a sort of doorkeeper, Uvani controlled access for the other spirits seeking to speak through Garrett.

A hallmark of Garrett's fifty-year career as a medium was a reputation for honesty. She never took money for her séances. And, though she worked in a time when spiritualism was under attack and many mediums were exposed as frauds, she remained beyond reproach. This is not to say, however, that her accuracy was beyond question. In fact, the results of one of her most famous mediumistic triumphs were subject to considerable debate.

The séance took place in London on October 7, 1930. It was organized by Harry Price, director of the National Laboratory of Psychic Research, who was one of three people seated at the séance table. By his side his secretary, a Miss Ethel Beenham, edged forward on her chair, her notebook poised, while an Australian newspaperman named Ian Coster nervously twined and unlaced his fingers. The evening had begun with talk about the most sensational current news. Two days before, the British dirigible R-101, the largest and costliest airship built to date, had crashed in northern France during its maiden voyage. In the ensuing explosions and fire, all but six of the fifty-four people on board perished. Among the dead was Flight Lieutenant Carmichael Irwin, the dirigible's commander. Newspapers bulged with accounts of the disaster, the worst in British aviation history at the time, and controversy raged over whether England's ambitious airship program should be jettisoned altogether.

The three séance participants had discussed the subject at some length, but now they were silent, all staring expectantly at the stylish woman slumped in an armchair. If her companions were almost feverishly anticipatory, she seemed unaware of it—or perhaps even bored by it. She was, as Coster later wrote, "yawning her head off."

The séance followed by three months the death of Sir Arthur Conan Doyle, the creator of Sherlock Holmes. A devout spiritualist, Conan Doyle was convinced that the living could commune with those who had crossed to the other side, as his fellow believers were wont to say. Thus it did not seem unreasonable to expect that he himself might be accessible post-mortem. So thinking, and sensing a possible sensational story, journalist Coster had asked Price to find the most reliable and respected medium in England to summon Conan Doyle's spirit. Price chose Eileen Garrett, the lady in the armchair.

Settling deeper into her cushion, Garrett breathed heavily and evenly, seeming to drift toward deep sleep. But no sooner had she closed her blue-green eyes than they began to gush tears, to the onlookers' astonishment. Uvani made only a brief appearance before an urgent voice interrupted him. "The whole bulk of the dirigible was . . . too much for her engine capacity," the male voice stuttered. The startled observers could see the psychic speaking, but the voice coming from her mouth certainly was not Garrett's, nor was it Uvani's, nor was it the restrained delivery of Conan Doyle. The speaker was agitated, panicky. "Useful lift too small," he said. "Gross lift computed badly . . . elevator jammed. Oil pipe plugged." On and on he went. Miss Beenham scribbled shorthand notes, her eyes glassy with amazement. Along with the others, she had read with horrified fascination the newspaper accounts of the R-101 disaster. No one had any trouble recognizing the man who was speaking through the medium. It seemed that Flight Lieutenant Irwin was describing in great technical detail the crash that had killed him two days before.

Sometime after Irwin finished his account, Conan Doyle did impart a message through Mrs. Garrett. At that point, however, the séance attendees regarded his contribution as a distinct anticlimax.

Garrett knew nothing about the mechanics of dirigibles, yet somehow she—or whoever was speaking through her—had spouted all sorts of technical aerodynamic details. Price rushed a transcript of the performance to the R-101's builders at the Royal Airship Works in Cardington. It was directed to a

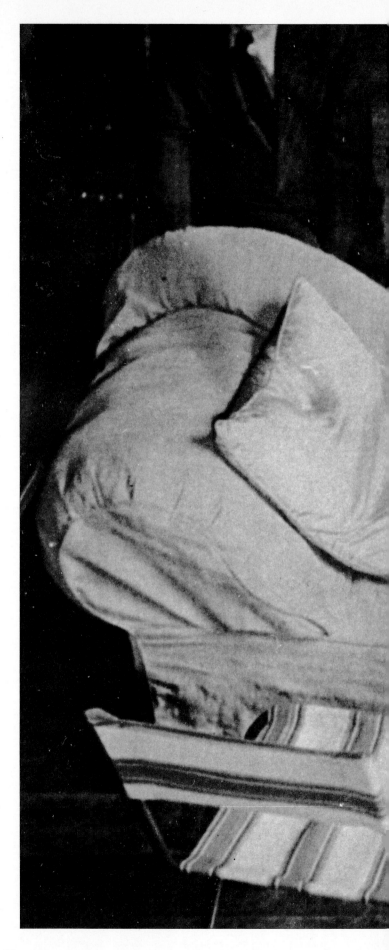

man named Charlton, described by Price as an "acclaimed expert" on the majestic zeppelin. The alleged expert declared himself astounded by the accuracy of Garrett's technical descriptions and her revelations of secret details about the airship. In fact, however, Charlton was not an engineer or an aviator, but one of 400 members of the Cardington ground crew. His expertise was thus much in question, as was his objectivity: He was, as it turned out, a spiritualist. When the same document Charlton had reviewed was shown to two high-ranking, well-qualified members of the airship team, they adjudged that most of the vaunted technical details that Garrett had spouted were dead wrong.

In addition, Charlton's contention that secret details came out at the séance was hard to credit, since virtually nothing about the R-101 was secret. The dirigible was a pet project of Britain's Labour party, then in power. The government, competing with a private company that was building a similar craft, was anxious to get the ship airborne to prove the superiority of state ownership over private enterprise. Thus bureaucrats were constantly dismissing objections from scientists that numerous technical problems had to be resolved before the zeppelin could safely fly. The whole matter became a subject of great public debate, and most anyone who cared to follow it in the newspapers knew almost all there was to know about the ill-fated R-101.

Nevertheless, Garrett's R-101 séance gained instant fame and easily outstripped the facts on its way to becoming legend. At the time, not even skeptics cared to call the lady a liar; her reputation was far too pristine. Rather, it was suggested that the medium had somehow picked up telepathic emanations from Coster, who, being a journalist, probably would have been familiar with at least some specifics about the dirigible and its problems. As was her habit, Garrett herself offered no assessment of the matter and left the debate about the séance to others.

Although her purported psychic gifts centered on mediumship, Garrett commonly experienced more straightforward psychic episodes as well. She was dining with friends at the Savoy Hotel in London one night during World War I when

she suddenly felt herself surrounded by reeking fumes and the sounds of war. At the same time, she had a horrifying clairvoyant vision of her young husband and several other men being blown up on a battlefield. A few days later, the British War Office advised her that her husband was among the missing. He had gone on a wire-cutting mission and not returned, and the War Office was never able to supply details of his death. "Only I knew the manner in which he had died," the psychic wrote at a later date.

Eileen Coley has said that her mother considered her unusual talents more a burden than a blessing, and her long search to explain them was a way of exorcising the affliction and trying to turn it to good use. "Why should she be stuck with this business, she felt, unless she could find out some way it could be used for the good of other human beings?" the daughter said. Garrett encouraged the laboratory approach to unraveling the mystery, as she encouraged all inquiry. But she observed that "any attempt to explain the

psyche and its manifold patterns in terms of language gets bogged down. The answer may well come from other aspects of science as yet not heard from officially." Finally, her quest was as inconclusive as it was thorough. It was not the habit of most mediums to doubt the utter veracity of their spirit guides, but Garrett, a lifelong skeptic despite her seeming gifts, was always dubious about the true nature of hers. In her autobiography, she theorized that the controls might have been no more than manifestations from her own subconscious. Beyond that, she knew of them only what she was told, she said, since she had never met them. Necessarily, they were present only when she was unconscious.

As to her purported powers of clairvoyance, telepathy, and precognition, Garrett was certain only that there was nothing supernatural, or even paranormal, about them. She speculated that they might have originated in the hypothalamus gland, or in the vestigial animal brain at the base of the skull. Animals seemed able to sense danger in ways unrelated to the five senses, she posited, while in most hu-

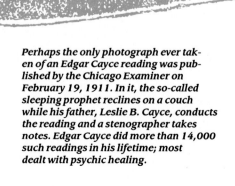

Perhaps the only photograph ever taken of an Edgar Cayce reading was published by the Chicago Examiner on February 19, 1911. In it, the so-called sleeping prophet reclines on a couch while his father, Leslie B. Cayce, conducts the reading and a stenographer takes notes. Edgar Cayce did more than 14,000 such readings in his lifetime; most dealt with psychic healing.

mans that knack might have atrophied beneath the weight of prodigious forebrains.

Secure in her powers but still unsure of their origins, Garrett died in France September 15, 1970, at the age of 77. Nearly two decades after her death, her Parapsychology Foundation still continued her work under Eileen Coley's stewardship. Coley's own daughter worked there as well, making three generations of Garrett women who had furthered efforts to chart the world of psychic powers.

Although Garrett and Edgar Cayce were contemporaries and had in common the apparent ability to transcend their own psyches, they could scarcely have been more different. Garrett was a brilliant, sophisticated, much-traveled, and worldly woman. Cayce was an unlettered rustic from rural Kentucky. Garrett spent a lifetime seeking to explore and develop her talents. Cayce was a somewhat reluctant seer, troubled through much of his life by his strange gifts. Cayce and Garrett met once, in the 1930s, and did readings for each other. Although associates of both said the psychics had great respect for each other, the single meeting did not produce a close friendship. Whatever the two may have had in common in matters of spirit, they were worlds apart in matters of style.

According to his biographers, Cayce's psychic turning point came on a fine May afternoon in 1890 when he was thirteen years old. He was sitting in the woods on the family farm near Hopkinsville, Kentucky, enjoying a favorite pastime—reading the Bible. Suddenly, he realized he was not alone. He looked up to see a woman standing before him. At first he thought it was his mother: The sun was bright behind her, and it was difficult to see. But when she spoke, he realized she was not anyone that he knew. Her voice was uncommonly soft and musical.

"Your prayers have been heard," she said. "Tell me what you would like most of all, so that I may give it to you."

Though frightened, the teenager stammered an answer: "Most of all I would like to be helpful to others, especially to children when they are sick."

Without reply the woman vanished into the sunbeams.

Edgar's first reaction was to fear he might be going crazy. But following on the heels of the vision was an indication that, indeed, he had been given some special power.

Edgar had never done well in school. His teachers complained that he was dreamy and inattentive. These failings much displeased his father, a no-nonsense fellow called Squire Cayce by his neighbors because he was the local justice of the peace. The night after the vision, Edgar was studying his spelling primer—as usual, without much luck—when the elder Cayce decided to take matters in hand. Father and son sat at a table with the book between them. Over the course of a long evening, the father intoned one word after another, and the son spelled most of them incorrectly. At half past ten, the boy heard the lady in the woods saying, "If you can sleep a little, we can help you." Begging the squire for a short respite, Edgar curled up in a chair with the spelling book under his head and fell asleep instantly.

When the lesson resumed a few minutes after he woke, the story goes, Edgar's answers were rapid and correct. To his father's astonishment, he went on to spell words from future lessons and even to specify which words were on which page and what illustrations went with them. For the rest of his life, Edgar Cayce allegedly maintained this clairvoyant ability to absorb near-photographic images of printed matter when, literally, he slept on it.

Not long after the spelling incident, young Edgar had an accident. In games during recess at school, a pitched ball hit him near the base of the spine. There was no apparent serious injury, but for the rest of the day he behaved oddly. At dinner that night, the normally reserved boy threw things at his three

sisters and taunted his father. Stranger yet, when he went to bed and fell asleep, he began to talk. He told his parents he was in shock. To cure it, he said, they should make a poultice of cornmeal, onions, and herbs, and apply it to the back of his head. They did. The next morning he remembered nothing at all of the day before, but he was back to normal. It seemed that he had just delivered his first psychic reading.

During the eleven years following these two curious episodes, Cayce made scant use of his apparent psychic power. He was ill at ease with it. A deeply religious fundamentalist Christian, he was unsure whether his gift came from God or the devil or why, in either case, it should have devolved on him. It is possible he might have continued trying to ignore his talents indefinitely had he not, in 1900, lost his voice.

It was a peculiar infirmity in that doctors found no apparent physical cause for it, yet it persisted into 1901. This came at a particularly troublesome time. Cayce was just starting to make his way as an apprentice photographer, hoping to earn enough money to marry his fiancée, Gertrude Evans. Being unable to talk above a muffled rasp was interfering with both his career and his courtship. Near despair, Cayce turned for a cure to hypnotism, which was much in vogue in the United States at the time.

A local hypnotist named Al C. Layne, familiar with the squire's tale of Edgar's poultice cure, proposed putting the younger Cayce into a trance and having him diagnose himself. Edgar agreed to try. On a Sunday afternoon in March, Layne was ushered into the parlor of the Cayce farmhouse, where the squire and Edgar waited. Layne began talking softly, try-

ing to induce a trance, but his patient interrupted. There was no need for such an effort, Edgar said. He often put himself "to sleep." It was no trouble at all. Layne should just concentrate on making the proper suggestions once Edgar was under. With that, the young man sighed deeply and slipped instantly into what appeared to be profound slumber. Layne then suggested that Edgar look inside his own body and pinpoint the trouble with his throat.

As his biographers would have it later, the entranced Cayce began to mumble at first, and then the young man began to speak in a clear voice. "Yes," he said, "we can see the body. In the normal state this body is unable to speak due to a partial paralysis of the inferior muscles of the vocal cords, produced by nerve strain. This is a psychological condition producing a physical effect. This may be removed by increasing the circulation to the affected parts by suggestion while in this unconscious condition."

The squire and the hypnotist were amazed. Edgar did not ordinarily talk that way. Awake, he might not have been able to pronounce some of those words, let alone understand them. Nevertheless, Layne gave the instructed suggestion. He and the squire looked on for the next twenty minutes while the skin over Edgar's throat and upper chest turned pink, then rose, then crimson with heightened blood flow. Finally, the sleeping man spoke.

"It is all right now," he said. "The condition is removed. Make the suggestion that the circulation return to normal, and that after that the body awaken." When Cayce awoke, his voice was fully restored.

Layne, who dabbled in osteopathy, argued that Cayce should use his apparent gift for psychic healing to help others. At first, Cayce resisted. He knew nothing about his unconscious pronouncements except what he was told, and certain-

ly he had no conscious control over them. He feared he might harm the very people he was trying to help. But finally, reluctantly, he agreed it was his duty to try.

Over the next twenty-two years, Cayce did thousands of medical readings. Twice a day he would lie down and "sleep," as he regarded it. In this altered state, which resembled a self-induced hypnotic trance, he would answer requests for psychic healing. As newspapers began spreading reports of his work, those requests began coming in from throughout the United States. Cayce dealt with as many of these requests as time permitted. Apparently, distance was no barrier to his alleged mental probes, since he often did readings for clients who were hundreds of miles away. In time he came to have thousands of enthusiastic supporters. But, of course, there were detractors as well.

A very private man, Cayce suffered under the notoriety his work occasioned, and he was mortified by the inevitable accusations of fraud. In November of 1931, during a brief visit to meet with admirers in New York, he ran afoul of the law. He had acceded to two women's request for a reading, but the women turned out to be police officers and Cayce was arrested. He was charged under a 1927 New York statute making it a misdemeanor to tell fortunes for money or with intent to defraud. At a hearing before a magistrate, Cayce was asked about claims that he was a psychic. "I make no claims whatever," he answered. "For thirty-one years I have been told I was a psychic. It first began as a child. I didn't know what it was. After it had gone on for years, a company was formed to study my work."

The company in question was the Association for Research and Enlightenment (ARE), founded by Cayce adherents earlier in 1931 to study and preserve his work. The magistrate, deciding that the ARE was an "incorporated ec-

clesiastical body," threw the case out of court. The police had no right, the magistrate stated, to tamper with the beliefs of an ecclesiastical body. Besides, he did not believe Cayce intended any fraud.

Despite the favorable outcome, the case was enough to exacerbate the psychic's considerable self-doubt and send him into a depression. As he had several times during his career, he wondered if his apparent psychic gifts were either valid or useful, and he considered giving up the work.

Cayce sometimes longed for the kind of widespread legitimacy that seemed to elude him for much of his lifetime, but he was unsure how to pursue it. Submitting himself to testing by parapsychologists had little appeal, since he had acquired an early and deep distrust of scientific inquiry.

In 1906, when he was living in Bowling Green, Kentucky, Cayce let a physician friend persuade him to give a reading before an audience that included other doctors. Once Cayce was unconscious, a debate arose in the audience about the exact nature of his condition. Some argued for self-hypnosis, others for trance or dream, still others for simple fakery. One doctor stuck a needle in Cayce's arms, hands, and feet to see how the psychic would react. When there was no response to that assault, another physician pushed a hatpin all the way through the sleeping man's cheek.

"He's hardened to all of that," said a third skeptic, who then took out a penknife and partially excised the nail from Cayce's left forefinger. There was still no indication of pain and no blood, but when Cayce awoke he was in agony. In a rare loss of temper he berated his tormentors and, before walking out, declared: "I'll never try to prove anything to any one of you again."

Cayce was at odds with most traditional physicians, largely because of his medical unorthodoxy. His adherents have assessed his diagnostic accuracy at eighty-five percent. However, that figure was arrived at in a random sampling of only about .5 percent of the available data. The therapies he prescribed were eclectic and hard to classify. They encompassed osteopathy, chemotherapy, hydrotherapy, nutrition, chiropractic, massage, and home remedies. Some of the therapies were decidedly bizarre. For example, when his wife, Gertrude, was diagnosed as having terminal tuberculosis, he ordered a regimen entailing a special diet, small doses of heroin, the application of a poultice made of crushed grapes, and sniffing apple brandy fumes from a charred wooden keg. She made a complete recovery.

However, not all of Cayce's psychic healing went so well, and some cases were demonstrable failures. For instance, he once gave a long diagnosis for a little girl suffering from leukemia and recommended a complicated dietary treatment. Unfortunately, the child had died the day before the reading was given—a fact Cayce somehow failed to divine. In another case, he advised the following recipe for an ailing male patient: Boil together wild cherry bark, sarsaparilla root, wild ginger, Indian turnip, wild ginseng, prickly ash bark, buchu, and mandrake root. Add grain alcohol and tolu balsam. Administer for ten days.

The efficacy of this odd nostrum was not to be tested. Again, as it turned out, the psychic was prescribing for a patient who had already died.

Still, many of Cayce's clientele did report remarkable cures and were more than happy to pay for them. Nevertheless, Cayce intensely disliked taking money in return for his services. Although he was often on the edge of penury himself, he began accepting fees regularly only when, in middle age,

Armed with birth dates and times, high-tech psychic Bettina Lee uses a computer to cast astrology charts for her clients. She uses her supposed psychic powers to interpret the charts.

he concluded that he was fated for his psychic work. Not until 1923 did he give up photography and all other attempts at business and begin devoting full time to the readings. Even then, he never refused petitioners because they lacked the wherewithal to pay for his services.

Cayce's career took on a new dimension that same year. The instigator of the change was Arthur Lammers, who was a wealthy printer from Dayton, Ohio. Lammers sought out Cayce for some readings, but he did not want answers to health problems. Rather, he asked about such things as esoteric astrology, the workings of the subconscious, and the nature of spirit and soul. He mentioned the mystery religions of Egypt and Greece and Tibet and the Jewish cabala, along with alchemy, yoga, and theosophy.

Cayce had only the faintest idea of what the man was talking about, and he was not at all sure he wanted to know more. Once again, he felt a threat to his fundamentalist Christianity. What if Lammers was leading him to sacrilege? Eventually, however, Cayce let himself be persuaded to work with Lammers. Lammers argued that the ideas of one God, of the need for human morality and brotherhood, were common to all the great metaphysical systems. If Cayce could clear up the confusion that reigned beyond those central tenets, then it was his duty to do it.

Cayce gave a reading for Lammers that began with astrology. Its end result, however, was to confirm the reality of reincarnation. Humans did, indeed, experience successive lifetimes for the purpose of perfecting their souls, the ultimate aim being the union of those souls with God.

In time, Cayce's consternation at his own pronouncement gave way to belief. Once he was able to reconcile the idea of reincarnation with his Christian faith, he enthusiastically added metaphysical readings to his purely physical ones. He developed what he called a life reading. Starting with astrological conditions of the subject's birth, the life reading

would then turn to several of the individual's alleged past incarnations. The aim of a life reading was to find information from past lives that would make one's present existence happier and more fruitful.

When he was unconscious, Cayce always spoke of himself in the third person, which augmented the impression of some strange bifurcation in his personality. Awake, the mild-mannered provincial had no explanation for his seeming magic. However, once, in his altered state, he gave this assessment of his psychic powers:

"Edgar Cayce's mind is amenable to suggestion, the same as all other subconscious minds, but in addition thereto it has the power to interpret to the objective mind of others what it acquires from the subconscious mind of other individuals of the same kind. The subconscious mind forgets nothing. The conscious mind receives the impression from without and transfers all thought to the subconscious, where it remains even though the conscious be destroyed."

Some analysts of Cayce's work have categorized his power as clairvoyance—an ability to see into bodies at a distance to diagnose ailments, as well as a talent for peering into the past and future. However, Cayce and his family saw it more as telepathy—mind-to-mind communication—but on a subconscious level. In addition, Cayce seemed to be saying that he could telepathically tap into the knowledge of some transcendental mind, perhaps akin to what psychologist Carl Jung called the collective unconscious.

Cayce himself described this cosmic mind pool as God's book of remembrance or the universal consciousness. He also used a term that would eventually be popularized by New Age psychics who came after him—the akashic records. The term was derived from the Hindu theosophical word *akasa,* referring to a primary creative principle of nature. The authoritative *Encyclopedia of Occultism and Parapsychology* gives the definition of the akashic records as "a kind of central fil-

ing system of all events, thoughts and actions impressed upon an astral plane, which may be consulted in certain conditions of consciousness." Events so recorded on the astral ether were thought to be "reanimated by mystics like a celestial television set."

It was Cayce's habit to have someone take notes during his readings. In the early years, the transcriptionist would be his father or his wife, but in 1923, he hired Gladys Davis as a full-time secretary. Thereafter, there was a verbatim record of all his work. When Edgar Cayce died in 1945, he left behind more than 14,000 recorded readings, the great majority dealing either with physical ailments or with past lives of his clients. All remain on file in Virginia Beach, Virginia, at the headquarters of the ARE, which continues to flourish under the aegis of his two sons.

The ARE today claims a membership of more than 30,000 people. Thousands more belong to many "Search for God" study groups that pursue Cayce's work. These are located on every continent in the world except Antarctica. Some one hundred books have been written about the sleeping prophet, and collectively they have sold more than twelve million copies. No psychic, not even Eileen Garrett, has ever approached Edgar Cayce in popular appeal.

That appeal cannot be explained fully in terms of the knowledge he claimed to tap, phenomenal though it was. Rather, his enduring influence seems more a product of the man himself, the waking Cayce—gentle, unassuming, much-beleaguered, and perfectly ordinary. If Mrs. Garrett was the grand doyenne of the psychic world, Cayce was its quintessential common man. He was, as his chief biographer, Thomas Sugrue, once commented, "just an American guy." Precisely because of his ordinariness, hundreds of thousands of people who were not rich or famous or well connected could identify with him. They believed that if a man like Cayce could somehow enter a mysterious world that was finer, loftier, and

saner than this one, and if a powerless man could call on great power, then maybe anybody could. Certainly, in his wake, many have tried.

By the mid-1980s, believers in psychic phenomena had become a majority in America; two-thirds of American adults reported to pollsters that they had experienced psychic events. Among these millions, some belong to that multifocused kaleidoscope of disparate beliefs and pursuits that is the New Age subculture.

New Agers have no central organization, hierarchy, or common dogma. Their interests are extraordinarily diverse. Some are mild adherents who practice holistic health or try honing their psi potential as a hobby. Others are dedicated practitioners who build lifestyles around ancient mystery religions or the pronouncements of disembodied spirits.

Although most New Agers share an interest in psychic powers, there is some disagreement within the movement over what the word *psychic* means. Does it stop with mind reading, remote viewing, and seeing the past and future? Or does it apply in some general sense to all things that are arcane, occult, or spiritual? Cayce looked to the word's Greek origin, *psyche,* or soul, and defined it as "spirit, soul, or the imagination of the mind," having to do with things "not understood from the physical, or material, or conscious mind." For the most part, it is in this cosmic sense that things psychic underpin the New Age.

What all New Agers share is a search for some metaphysical meaning in life. In addition, most believe in the possi-

bility of transcending the mundane world in one way or another, whether by meditating on crystals or by studying with gurus or by any number of other vehicles.

Although detractors tend to regard them as holdover hippies or dwellers on the social fringe, New Agers hardly fit that profile. Neither are they a credulous, ignorant undercaste. SRI International estimated in 1987 that movement members made up some five to ten percent of the American population and that most were in their thirties or forties, affluent, and well educated. Especially in the cities, having a personal psychic adviser had become as chic for young professionals as driving the proper car or maintaining an exclusive address.

Thousands of enthusiasts have joined self-help groups, which operate toward the conservative end of the New Age spectrum and are akin to the so-called human potential movements popular in the 1970s. For instance, the Spiritual Frontiers Fellowship in New York sponsors lectures, seminars, and workshops on developing spirituality. The Fellowship, which utilizes the teachings of Cayce, among others, believes that psychic powers are often a by-product of the spiritual quest. Headquartered in Sedona, Arizona, a nonprofit organization called Free Soul seeks to explore the human spirit by means of biofeedback, meditation, and mind and body control. One aim is to cultivate psychic sensitivity for use in daily living. Free Soul has upward of two hundred instructors working throughout the United States and a clientele of approximately 25,000 people. Each pays ten dollars per lesson for the Free Soul instruction.

Some organizations offer almost limitless options for psi buffs. In New York City the Open Center, the Circle of Light Institute, and the Learning Annex provide past-life regressions, aura reading, and even telepathic communion with the psychic energy of whales. Venice, California, is headquarters

for the Conscious Connection, once a metaphysical meeting ground for single men and women but now open to all. It features the full psychic menu, but for the truly venturesome—skeptics might say the truly credulous—the Connection touts its centerpiece subgroup, the Channeling Network.

Channelers—the term has supplanted *mediums*—are a New Age passion. They purport to be pipelines for disembodied spirits, whether of long-dead humans or entities who never lived on this earthly plane. The Channeling Network offers a selection of channelers to accommodate the needs of a varied, but generally well-to-do, clientele. One of this number is Shawn Randall, who hosts a spirit adviser called Torah. Torah is described as an "interdimensional consciousness," and, according to Randall, is "a pretty easy guy to talk with." Torah regresses Randall's clients through past lives and, like most good spirits affiliated with channelers, gives advice on temporal problems. Some channelers specialize in dead celebrities. California-based William Tenuto claims to produce the late Beatle John Lennon, not to mention Jesus Christ. Tenuto says he has channeled Jesus often enough to call him "a good friend."

Channeling is a growth industry, complete with agents. New York's Cosmic Contact Psychic Services, the first agency to represent so-called paranormal professionals, includes channelers along with its more traditional astrologers, palmists, and tarot readers. Perhaps the most successful channeling entrepreneur, however, is a strictly freelance one-time homemaker from Yelm, Washington, named J. Z. Knight. Her claim to superterrestrial contact is as conduit for Ramtha, purportedly a 35,000-year-old warrior from the lost continent of Lemuria. Ramtha is quite a draw. In a husky voice that affects a variety of accents, he addresses large crowds in weekend seminars that cost $400 per person. The message is consistent with much New Age teaching: Everyone bears God within; there is no right or wrong, just individual reality; each person has the power to control his or her destiny. Knight's own destiny is getting along handsomely. Her income from Ramtha-related enterprises is said to run into the millions of dollars.

An estimated 2,500 New Age bookstores exist in America, and many New Age periodicals are available. Some specialize in networking information—about local witchcraft covens, for example. Some publications report heavily on personal mystical experiences. One popular magazine features interviews with dead celebrities.

The periodicals usually contain advertisements for all manner of occult talismans and psychic services. They tout books offering to reveal the ritual secrets of "Hopi sacred sweats" or detail the afterlives of plane-crash victims or teach the laws governing psychic assassinations. Psychics advertise to tap the universal consciousness for answers to petitioners' questions—all by mail and at the rate of only two dollars per answer, sometimes less.

These mail-order psychics occupy the low end of a psychic adviser hierarchy that is part of the New Age. Today, several hundred thousand psychic advisers are operating in the United States alone. Joining the mail-order contingent near the bottom of the scale are the old-style fortune tellers who use tea leaves or crystal balls, many of whom operate from shabby store fronts in the cities or from house trailers in the countryside. But there is also a new aristocracy of psychic advisers who are a far cry from the turbaned swamis or bejeweled gypsies of popular folklore. The new seers dress tastefully, live well, and command large fees from large followings. Some attract celebrity clients, and some of them are celebrities in their own right. Whether these advisers read tarot cards or astrology charts, they usually come equipped with business cards and press kits.

One such representative of the psychic elite is Patricia McLaine of Arlington, Virginia, just across the Potomac River from the capital city of Washington. Around four or five times each weekday, McLaine will sit with one of her clients in the sunny study of her suburban home and lay out the tarot cards that help guide her readings. She is not, however, always in residence there. She travels often to serve people in Texas and California. There are still other clients as far away as Europe, Asia, and Australia, with whom she confers by telephone. In all, she estimates that she has as many as 3,000 clients, most of whom, she says, come in for "a yearly checkup or a twice-a-year checkup." Her patrons include a number of well-known individuals, among them actress Shirley MacLaine, whose best-selling books and popular television movie about her own metaphysical search prompted a boomlet within the New Age movement. Featured in several books and magazine articles about psychics, Patricia McLaine is also a popular television talk-show guest.

Utilizing astrology as well as tarot, she usually gives readings that last for a half hour or an hour. She charges $65 for the shorter reading, $125 for the longer. In addition, her more affluent clients might request a master reading, which lasts several hours. The master reading, for which McLaine prepares with meditation and fasting in order to achieve a properly receptive state of mind, covers a sitter's past lives and the numerous intricate relationships that may be affecting the present existence.

"I don't think I would have become a psychic if I hadn't

A black orb of Venetian crystal figures in John Christopher Travers's readings, along with the tarot cards and a magnifying glass he uses to read the fine lines in his clients' hands.

started reading Edgar Cayce books in the 1960s," McLaine says. In those days, she was an aspiring young playwright working as a secretary at the Twentieth Century Fox movie studio in Los Angeles. Inspired by what she read of Cayce, she began visiting psychics. After two of them told her that she herself would eventually become a psychic reader, she began doing free readings for her friends at the studio. McLaine's career developed from there.

She classifies herself as partly psychic but "at least 50 percent intuitive." There is, she says, a big difference. "The intuitive is superior to the psychic," she explains. "The psychic is receiving a feeling or an impression, and the intuitive level of knowledge is direct knowledge." A psychic impression is like "looking at something through a foot of water. You may see it correctly, you may not . . . or maybe you get a general impression, but it may not be the absolute." With intuition, though, one "can't be wrong."

Whatever her vehicle of access may be, McLaine describes the source of her psychic knowledge as "the great storehouse of the collective unconscious. That's where it all comes from. That's where it is created. People are creating their lives at all moments of all days. The psychic person is simply able to tune in to that."

Despite her success, McLaine has misgivings about her vocation. A serious student of metaphysics for more than twenty years, she began in 1975 to teach courses on tarot, the cabala, and other metaphysical subjects. She prefers teaching these subjects to being what she calls "an esoteric psychologist" for her clients. People are inclined to vest too much power in their psychic advisers, she says, rather than work toward enlightenment on their own.

"A lot of people are not willing to meditate and put the effort into spiritual study that is involved in developing your higher connection," she says. "They want it to be real easy and simple—'show me the fastest way to heaven.' There's one

creative process, and we are godlets. A master of wisdom would not sit down and read your cards for you, or do your planets for you, or give you a reading. He would try to give you principles by which to live in order to enhance your life."

McLaine attributes the modern psychic and spiritual revival to the fact that the so-called Age of Aquarius, which dawned in the 1960s, is just picking up steam in the 1980s. She hails the Aquarian Age, a term that is synonymous with the New Age, as a time of great spiritual awakening and evolution. Nevertheless, she acknowledges that not all psychics are equally talented—nor are they equally honest. "A lot of people in my business," she says, "are downright strange."

Indeed, debunkers of psychics pinpoint several techniques used by the dishonest to bilk clients. Chief among these is the so-called cold reading in which the psychic is able to satisfy a client by tossing out generalities and then detecting responses *(page 102)*. Part of the cold reading is the "stock spiel," wherein the sitter is offered a set of bland pronouncements that could apply to almost anyone. In many cases, the sitter's reactions to the spiel, both verbal and in body language, cue the alert reader to home in on a few particulars— enough, often, to convince the sitter that he or she has experienced a true psychic event.

Most well-known psychics of recent years have provided some psychic counseling for individual clients, but not all have specialized in it. For example, Chicago's Irene Hughes, although she is an adviser for several celebrities, is probably better known as a seer in the realm of public events. Among the more notable of her claimed precognitions were the assassinations of John and Robert Kennedy and Martin Luther King, Jr., the 1967 outbreak of the Arab-Israeli Six Day War, and President Lyndon B. Johnson's decision not to seek a second term. A popular television personality and newspaper columnist, the platinum-haired psychic was born Irene Finger in rural Tennessee, one of eleven children in a poor farm family. As a child, her feelings about incipient events supposedly proved accurate enough to prompt her father to consult her about when to pick cotton or when to expect rain.

Harking back to psychic superstars of an earlier generation, Hughes shared with Edgar Cayce a sylvan vision in childhood and with Eileen Garrett an Oriental spirit guide. When she was four, Hughes was alone in the woods when she allegedly was visited by a shimmering lady. The luminous vision described and validated the child's ability to feel strange and wonderful things not sensed by others. Some years later, the adult Hughes was recovering from surgery when she received another visit from a discarnate entity. As she lay at home in her sickbed, an Oriental man materialized in front of her and identified himself as Kaygee.

As Hughes later reported the conversation that followed, Kaygee described himself as "your control, your teacher, and your friend." He predicted that she would eventually learn "many things unknown to others" and would have "the key to all life." During the course of their meeting, Hughes said, Kaygee guided her through her incarnation in a past life in Egypt. Kaygee was supposedly a wise Japanese Christian who died in 1961. A devout Christian herself, Hughes considers her psychic abilities to be God-given.

Hughes is among many psychics who believe psychic talent is present, at least potentially, in everyone. But New York's Alex Tanous thinks himself uniquely marked from birth with signs of special gifts. Tanous is of Lebanese extraction, and his father was a friend of the famed Lebanese poet Kahlil Gibran. By the psychic's account, Gibran predicted to the elder Tanous before Alex's birth that the boy would become "a man of exceptional gifts, of great abilities." In addition, Tanous says, he was born with some lines in his palm forming a hexagram and others depicting a mystic cross, and still others spelling the name "Alex" backward. He was also born with a

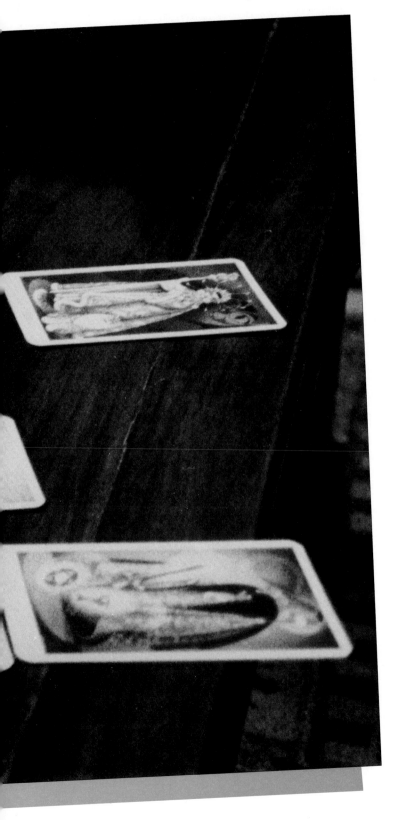

A London psychic lays out tarot cards in one of the many formations used in divination.

caul, a fetal membrane that covered his face. In several cultures the caul signifies second sight. Like most psychics, Tanous believes his gifts were manifest in childhood. Retrocognition was one of them. In school, he did well in history, he says, because he was able to return in time and relive whatever period was under study.

Among the most intriguing of Tanous's seeming paranormal aspects is the special relationship he claims to have with light. He energizes himself psychically, he says, by looking into bright lights, even into the sun. Although he recommends against others trying the technique, he reports that he himself has never suffered the retinal burns that might be expected to result. Moreover, Tanous's mysterious connection with light apparently encompasses transmitting as well as receiving. He can, according to some witnesses, make balls of light shoot out of his eyes.

Such extravagant claims meet considerable skepticism, of course. Nor are New Age paths to enlightenment always viewed with equanimity. The critics' responses range from mild to vitriolic. Some psychologists see the movement as a fairly innocuous attempt by people who are disillusioned with organized religion to fill a spiritual vacuum in their lives. "Many well-educated people have moved away from traditional religion," says Dr. Robert Millman of Cornell Medical College, an expert in social psychiatry. "But they still want to believe there is a force that is higher than themselves; they don't want to think they are insignificant little animals, produced by a random series of events. They want to know that there is a system, and they want to know where they fit in." Others, those who are wary of the cultlike aspect of some New Age phenomena, regard the movement as far more dangerous. A West German psychologist, describing an "occult epidemic" in his country, says teenagers are suffering mental health problems from contact with occult practices.

In one reported case in the United States, belief in a psychic's prediction proved deadly to a susceptible adult. A Colorado woman, upon being told by a medium that she and a married man for whom she cared would become lovers

Is This the Real You?

You are basically a serious person, but with a fine sense of humor. A loner by temperament, you nevertheless have a talent for working with others. You prefer people whose intellects equal yours, but you are never unkind to inferiors. You are very sensitive but tend to maintain a stiff upper lip in difficult times. You sometimes feel insecure, but you mask it so well that friends see you as confident and outgoing. You are meticulous — a perfectionist — but an overabundance of details bores you. You crave adventure but are never irresponsible. You have a complex nature and wide-ranging interests, coupled with a great ability to focus all your energies on a single task.

Does this description fit you? It should. It fits most people; or, at least, it fits the self-image of most people. Hardly anyone with a well-integrated ego cares to think of himself or herself as a frivolous, humorless, ignorant, insensitive, weak, boring, shallow clod. Any good psychic reader knows this; thus, a so-called cold reading — such as the one you just read — will almost always be flattering as well as general. It will also offer choices. Note that most of the propositions paired above are basically contradictory. Nevertheless, a psychic's client — generally known as a sitter — will tend to integrate them into a coherent statement. Moreover, the more intelligent the sitter, the more complete this integration is apt to be. Humans process all sensory input by imposing order on chaos, and they will usually react to a psychic reading no differently. And if you come down on one side of a reader's equation harder than on the other, well and good. Verbally or with body language, you will probably give the psychic enough clues to move from generalities to particulars.

Also operating in this situation is a phenomenon called subjective validation. This means that you tend to make the reader's statements fit in with what you already know or believe about yourself. In this way, the sitter may do most of the real work in a reading, interpreting the adviser's vague generalities as personally tailored revelations.

in a future life, killed the man and then committed suicide. Much criticism centers on speculation about fraud. "A lot of people get in to make money and pass themselves off as having supernatural powers," says Marc Medoff, publisher of *Whole Life* magazine, which deals with New Age topics. "We get complaints all the time from people who are charged a lot for rubbish that's made up on the spot." Jacob Needleman, a theologian at the University of California at Berkeley, notes there is "no Better Business Bureau" in the psychic world. "Let the buyer beware," he says. "You should be open-minded, but not so open-minded that your brains fall out."

In the main, the New Age is anathema to conventional religion. Some religious leaders see it as a kind of collective antichrist. Others simply deplore its depersonalization of God, with the concomitant notion that "anything is permissible if everything is God." "When people stop believing in God, they'll believe in anything," says Reverend Monsignor William B. Smith, academic dean and professor of moral theology at St. Joseph's Seminary in Yonkers, New York. "We start relying on ersatz substitutes: crystal balls, tarot cards. One is as irrational as the next, and none can determine your free will or your future." Even so, a New Age influence can be discerned in mainstream religion: an upswing in faith healing among Episcopalians, a revival of Jewish mysticism, the training of meditation in Roman Catholic monastaries.

It is doubtful that the New Age, in all its varied aspects, would have won unqualified approval from its precursors. Edgar Cayce and Eileen Garrett probably would have applauded the search for spiritual elevation. But, without question, Cayce would have been appalled by the New Age departure from traditional religion and the enthusiastic neopaganism. As for Eileen Garrett, Eileen Coley said her mother would have regarded much of the New Age as "utter nonsense."

Nevertheless, it was one of Mrs. Garrett's fondest hopes that her own work with psychic phenomena would hasten the time when people would find practical uses for such powers. Perhaps she would have been gratified to know that as the New Age dawned, pragmatists both within it and outside it were trying to do exactly that.

Psychics at Center Stage

T he title psychic has been given to a diverse collection of characters, from medieval soothsayers to the unlettered Edgar Cayce. But nowhere has the word aroused more ire than in the field of stage magic. Professional magicians, or conjurers, usually have individual specialties. Illusionists cause large objects to appear or vanish (or so it seems); escape artists free themselves from seemingly inextricable bonds. Mentalists, the psychics of the stage, perform feats of apparent telepathy or clairvoyance, but some outrage fellow entertainers by claiming to have real psychic powers.

When believers in psychic phenomena point to these performers as living evidence of the paranormal, skeptics — many of them professional magicians — retort that mentalists such as Uri Geller and George Kresge, known as Kreskin, are nothing more than glorified tricksters, exploiting a gullible public. For their part, mentalists take a philosophical view: Just because psychic powers resist laboratory testing or can be copied by clever magicians is no reason to believe that such phenomena do not exist. The controversy began more than a century ago — and is not likely to end soon.

The Mind Who Came to Dinner

On May 12, 1889, a pale young man stood before a gathering at the exclusive Lambs Club of New York City. His goal: nothing less than to provide conclusive proof of his ability to read minds. Yet, despite supposed psychic gifts that had attracted worldwide attention, the thirty-three-year-old mentalist apparently did not foresee that this demonstration, the crowning event of his career, would have a gruesome finale.

Washington Irving Bishop was not any stranger to controversy. In the early 1880s, he had created a sensation with his Blindfold Carriage Test, a dramatic demonstration of what he termed mental telegraphy. Donning a heavy black hood and taking the reins of a horse-drawn cart, Bishop led a mob of 500 news reporters and spectators on a wild ride through midtown Manhattan as he tracked down a hidden diamond brooch—solely, he said, by the power of thought. Later, on a headline-making tour of Europe, the mentalist apparently read the thoughts of the Prince of Wales in order to locate a gold sovereign coin concealed in the Duchess of Kent's silk stocking. On that same tour, however, the young performer found himself at odds with an established magician, John Nevil Maskelyne, who claimed Bishop was a trickster without genuine powers. After a heated exchange of accusations, Bishop thought it prudent to leave Britain.

Returning to the United States, Bishop met more opposition. In New York, a promi-

Just months before his death, mind reader Washington Irving Bishop flaunts the medals he claimed to have received from the crowned heads of Europe.

Magician Jean Eugène Robert-Houdin and son Emile perform a second-sight act in 1848.

nent newspaper editor published his own explanation of many of Bishop's most prized thought-reading effects. Bishop, said the editor, was nothing more than a glorified magician. Although the performer steadfastly maintained that his demonstrations were genuine, the accusation seriously tarnished his reputation and left him more determined than ever to prove himself a genuine psychic. The Lambs Club afforded him an opportunity to restore his good name. When a friend invited him to dine, Bishop knew that the evening would provide an ideal platform for his talents.

After the meal was finished, the Lambs Club members—many of whom were show people themselves—clamored for a demonstration of thought reading. Bishop happily obliged them. A high-strung, agitated performer, he fairly quivered as he announced that he would favor the assembly with an effect that he had recently exhibited for the tsar of Russia. Before leaving the room in the company of a club member, Bishop asked that an imaginary murder scene be enacted in his absence, complete with a killer, a victim, a weapon, and a witness. The chosen killer, whose identity Bishop would not know, was instructed to select a victim, then act out a crime of his own devising, and finally hide the weapon.

This was done, and the members called Bishop back into the room with his chaperone, who attested that the mind reader could not have heard or seen anything that oc-

curred in his absence. The mentalist set to work with characteristic energy. Allowing a blindfold to be fastened over his eyes, he took the arm of a witness and began pacing furiously. To the astonishment of all, Bishop unhesitatingly identified the killer and victim and located the hidden murder weapon.

The feat won warm applause, but the mentalist was far from finished. By now Bishop's nerves seemed at the breaking point; trembling hands and ashen features attested to the enormous strain of his efforts, but he seemed determined to press on.

Clay Green, the Lambs Club secretary, volunteered to help Bishop in his next feat. Bishop asked Green to focus all his thought on a book listing Lambs Club members. When he could picture it clearly in his mind, Bishop instructed, Green was to select a name found in its pages.

Again donning his heavy blindfold, Bishop grasped the secretary by the arm and led him on a frantic dash through the building, knocking over tables and chairs until—still blindfolded—the mentalist laid his hands on the register book Green had envisioned.

This demonstration of thought reading won more enthusiastic applause from the observers, but Bishop was not finished. Holding up a hand for silence, the performer announced that he would reveal—by probing Green's innermost thoughts—the name selected moments earlier. Bishop still clutched Green by the arm. His features contorted with effort; a series of groans escaped

his lips. Finally, his hands jerking spasmodically, he seized a pen and pad and scrawled a puzzling message:

TOWNSEND

Nonplussed, Green revealed that he had chosen the name Margaret Townsend from the membership rolls. When he held the message up to a mirror, the name TOWNSEND was dramatically revealed.

Even as the audience exploded into applause, Bishop's exertions caught up with him. The performer pulled off his blindfold and crumpled to the floor. Stunned club members put him to bed in an upstairs room, and a doctor in attendance attempted to revive Bishop with electric shocks and injections of brandy. Not surprisingly, by the time morning arrived he was unconscious and was soon pronounced dead.

This was not the first time such a thing had happened to Bishop. The young man suffered from catalepsy, a condition characterized by sudden plunges into an unconsciousness so deep that all life signs were supressed. Often the stresses of his performances would bring seizures upon him. Indeed, Bishop had been pronounced dead on two previous occasions, only to recover unaided several hours later.

There would be no such recovery after the Lambs Club episode. Convinced that the mentalist was dead, a doctor from New York Hospital immediately performed an autopsy, removing his brain. Bishop's distraught mother arrived too late to prevent the action. Ever afterward she maintained that her son had been murdered by medical ghouls, eager to learn the secrets of Bishop's powers.

Trade Secrets

Ironically, the man who had risen to fame as "the world's first and world eminent mind reader" began his career as the scourge of spiritualism. In 1876, capitalizing on secrets learned as an assistant to Anna Eva Fay, a famous American medium, Bishop developed a popular stage program in which he re-created—and then exposed—the most cherished routines of professional mediums.

A feature of this act, and one that Bishop insisted was genuine, was a demonstration of thought reading. However, Bishop's thought-reading stunts, which he advanced as evidence of superior powers, took their inspiration from a world-renowned magician—a man who made no claim whatsoever to psychic gifts.

Jean Eugène Robert-Houdin, a French clockmaker turned conjurer, had stunned Parisian audiences in the 1840s with his seemingly supernatural second-sight act. His performance was straightforward enough, but it had a dazzling effect. While the magician circulated among his audience, his young son Emile sat blindfolded on the stage. As audience members handed Robert-Houdin small items from their pockets or handbags, the magician asked his son to identify them. Emile would then shout out astonishingly complete descriptions, as if—though blindfolded—he could plainly see the objects. No detail escaped the magician's son; he could even be counted on to recite the contents of private letters or read the foreign-language inscriptions on medallions and coins that were proffered.

The second-sight act, which relied on an ingenious and elaborate verbal code understood only by the magician and his son, proved ill-suited to the plans of Washington Irving Bishop, who preferred to work alone. Accordingly, Bishop traded the secrets he gleaned from Robert-Houdin's memoirs to a resourceful mentalist named J. Randall Brown. In return, Brown taught Bishop the technique that would come to make him famous. Brown's technique, known today as muscle reading, is itself very nearly as incredible as the seemingly psychic feats it enabled Bishop to perform. Only a handful of mentalists over the last century have mastered this delicate, inexact skill, which depends on unconscious physical indicators given by an innocent volunteer. In a typical case, the performer of muscle reading will ask his subject, usually a member of the audience, to concentrate on an object hidden nearby. Then, gripping the arm or wrist of the subject, the muscle reader begins to move about the room, asking for mental commands leading to the hidden object, such as "go forward" or "turn left."

With enough practice, the performer becomes sensitive to tiny movements by the subject that are imperceptible to the audience. For example, if the subject gives a slight pulse of resistance, the performer realizes he is heading the wrong way. If there is no resistance, the direction is correct. Thus, even when blindfolded, a stage mentalist using this technique can locate a hidden object as long as he is touching someone who knows where the object is. A canny performer can very easily give the appearance of reading minds.

Bishop relied heavily on muscle reading as he molded himself into one of the nineteenth century's most remarkable performers. So great was his success that by the time of his unfortunate death in 1889, public exhibitions of thought reading had become almost commonplace.

Psychics under the Big Top

Although Bishop's career had ended, the public's appetite for demonstrations of psychic powers remained very much alive. A host of colorful Bishop imitators emerged in

Eleanor Bishop hovers over the lifeless body of her son, who by 1889 had become the world's foremost thought reader. An autopsy line across the deceased mentalist's forehead attests to the unfortunate circumstances of his death.

A lithograph advertises the young Harry Houdini's skill as a card manipulator without mentioning the mentalism act that the magician sometimes performed on the same bill.

Despite his success, Houdini remained ambivalent about his career as a mentalist. In 1898, he decided to abandon the act, claiming that if he could not make good as a real magician within a year, he would find himself a more respectable job.

Anna Eva Fay, considered the greatest female stage psychic of all time, shared none of Houdini's reservations about her chosen career. Fay was an accomplished magician who turned to mentalism in the 1870s, giving séances in music halls and variety shows. By the time of her retirement in 1924, she had risen to the status of a vaudeville headliner. Described as "a slender, almost fragile creature with grey eyes and flaxen hair," the psychic invariably made a most bewildering impression on her audiences.

In the centerpiece of Fay's act, the mentalist sat on the stage, blindfolded and covered by a thick orange sheet, as she answered unspoken questions from the audience. At the start of ev-

ery performance, she explained that in order for her to form a clear psychic impression, each question must be written out on a pad of paper. Participants then ripped off the top sheet and Fay's assistants collected the unused portion of the pads. Almost immediately, the mentalist would begin calling out answers from beneath her sheet.

Ironically, it was Washington Irving Bishop, a former assistant, who exposed her ingenious secret—though her career seemed unaffected by Bishop's revelations. In an

Magician James S. Harto — also known as Chandra — and his wife, Verda Wren, affected exotic silk robes to capitalize on the demand for mystical thought-reading acts.

the 1890s, many of them magicians whose careers had hit the skids. These performers, of widely varying skill and credibility, permeated the circuses, "dime museums," and variety halls of the day, often vanishing from public view as quickly as they had appeared. Those who managed to duplicate Bishop's effects could seldom match his attention-grabbing histrionics—except perhaps for Theodore Pull, whose gimmick of chewing on a piece of soap during his performances gave the impression that psychic fervor caused him to foam at the mouth.

Even Harry Houdini, later the most vehement antispiritualist of his generation, served a brief early turn as a psychic entertainer. Known at the turn of the century as Dime Museum Harry, owing to the seedy venues in which he appeared, Houdini brought the same flair to his mind-reading act that he would later apply to his career as an escape artist. Transmitting coded signals to his wife, Bess, with almost imperceptible wiggles of his right ear, Houdini could stage a convincing display of mentalism. When, on one occasion, he appeared to be delivering messages from a local murder victim, superstitious audience members fled from the theater in panic.

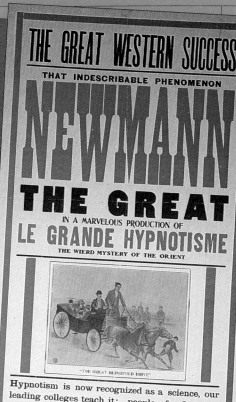

C. A. George Newmann performed his act in a way that confounded all as to the secret of his blindfold carriage ride. As shown here, he gripped the horses' reins, not his volunteer's wrist.

anonymous newspaper article published early in both performers' careers, Bishop revealed that as Fay's spectators wrote their questions on the note pads provided, a thin coating of paraffin on the second sheet took an impression of the pencil markings. Backstage, her assistants quickly dusted the paraffin with graphite, yielding a clear copy of the questions while the originals remained in the hands of the audience. The assistants then transmitted these questions to Fay through a speaking tube that ran through a hole drilled in the stage floor.

Having taken such extraordinary measures to discern her audience's questions, Fay was scarcely less clever in devising the answers. Generally the questions held simple pleas for advice, but Fay proved herself equal to greater challenges. On one occasion late in her career, a Brooklyn man asked where his stolen car might be found. Pausing dramatically and giving appropriate gasps of effort from beneath her orange covering, the performer slowly recited an address. The next day's newspapers reported that the missing automobile had indeed been found at that exact location. As the city buzzed with the news of Fay's stunning feat, an energetic reporter uncovered a disillusioning piece of information. Fay's husband had paid two men to steal the car and park it in a prearranged location. Simple theft, not psychic illumination, had brought about the miracle.

Such revelations did little to dampen the public's enthusiasm for mentalism on the stage. Another stage psychic, Stuart Cumberland, claimed that more than 1,000 scientists and members of the clergy had endorsed his powers as genuine. Along with thought reading, Cumberland regaled his audiences with tales of having read the best minds of the era, including those of British statesman William E. Gladstone and Kaiser Wilhelm II of Germany.

Even Fannie Brice, the popular comedic star of the Ziegfeld Follies, was known to entertain her friends with amateur mind-reading stunts. Asked for an explanation, she replied, rather obliquely, "Oh, I just do these things, darling."

Minds of the Times

As the demand grew for psychic entertainment, the techniques used by Bishop and others became more widely known to the public. Audiences familiar with codes and muscle reading demanded more sophisticated feats before they would consider a psychic genuine.

Maude Lancaster, an English woman, demonstrated one great procedural improvement. In 1893, while performing the familiar stunt of locating a hidden object, Lancaster succeeded without physical contact of any kind. Although blindfolded, she also duplicated Bishop's murder-mystery test and several other impressive stunts, all without benefit of touch.

Lancaster's success prompted many to proclaim her a genuine psychic, but in fact she was one of the first to use a technique that soon came to be called noncontact thought reading. This method of achieving seemingly psychic results relied mainly on a keen visual interpretation of the same physical clues felt by the earlier muscle readers.

Joseph Mercedes and Mademoiselle Stantone combined thought reading with piano playing in a "mental novelty" act one critic called "the acme of finesse."

To be successful with this highly delicate approach, a performer needed sharp eyes, hours of practice, and—in many cases—a see-through blindfold.

C. A. George Newmann may have had all of these things and more. The Minnesota-bred mentalist, whose long career spanned the years from the late 1890s into the 1950s, even one-upped Washington Irving Bishop's famous blindfolded carriage rides. Unlike his predecessor, who took the reins in one hand and the wrist of his helper in the other, Newmann would keep both hands on the reins of his carriage, while the person who had hidden the search object remained in the back seat. Even if he was aided by the noncontact technique, it seems as if Newmann must have had eyes in the back of his head to succeed in this dramatic display; his

The thought-transference act of Julius Zancig and his wife, Agnes, impressed even Houdini, who admitted "I have failed to trace anyone superior."

secret has never been revealed to the public.

Not all stage mentalists relied on such techniques. A phenomenal act from the 1920s and 1930s called "Mercedes and the Marvelous Musical Mystic Mademoiselle Stantone" had its roots in the verbal deception of the illustrious Robert-Houdin. In this act, Joseph Mercedes moved among his audience, encouraging spectators to whisper the names of popular tunes into his ear. Almost at once, the blindfolded Mademoiselle Stantone, seated at a piano on stage, would play the chosen selections.

This act fooled not only the pair's vast audiences but also magicians familiar with Robert-Houdin's word code. The performers spoke very little during their act, and what they said varied only slightly from night to night. Could this at last be a demonstration of actual psychic power on stage?

The solution proved less mystical, though

nearly as impressive. Rather than rely on a spoken code, Mercedes had devised a system based on the length of the pauses between his words to communicate the selected tunes. Thus, even while Mademoiselle Stantone played a brisk fox trot or languorous waltz, the two performers remained synchronized by a private tempo counted off silently to themselves.

Stage mentalists continued to entrance audiences through the first decades of the twentieth century, even as the exact nature of their art grew more controversial. No two figures more clearly embodied the opposing sides of that debate than the distinguished writer Sir Arthur Conan Doyle, an avid spiritualist, and the zealously skeptical Harry Houdini. Although fast friends, the two men found themselves at odds over the mind-reading capabilities of Danish performers Julius and Agnes Zancig.

In an act entitled "Two Minds with a Single Thought," Zancig and his wife appeared to read each other's mind as well as minds in the audience. The pair generated such interest that within a few years of their debut in 1892 they commanded the most exclusive stages in show business, including an eleven-week engagement at Oscar Hammerstein's famed Roof Garden in New York City. One journalist was so moved by the Zancigs' seeming ability to read and transmit thoughts that he wrote: "It is a case of telepathy pure and simple. The respective mental batteries of this pair are so perfectly adjusted that the vibration of the thought current of the man instantly registers itself upon the mind of the wife."

Conan Doyle echoed this opinion. After seeing the Zancigs' act in 1922, the creator of Sherlock Holmes commented: "I am quite assured that their remarkable performance, as I saw it, was due to psychic causes [thought transference] and not to trickery."

The British author, renowned for the rigid logic and keen reasoning of his fictional detective, was an uncritical supporter of psychic claims, and he spent the final years of his life in enthusiastic pursuit of paranormal phenomena. In his passion, Conan Doyle would often proclaim mediums and psychics to be genuine even when other observers could easily provide more mundane explanations of their feats.

Houdini, despite his own early turn as a mentalist, had become the world's foremost exposer of fraudulent mediums, tirelessly attending performances and séances in order to confront phony spiritualists. In fact, many of the conjurer's own performances were given over to the exposure of mediums whom he believed to be bilking the public of hard-earned money.

In his book *A Magician among the Spirits*, Houdini commented on Conan Doyle's fascination with the Zancigs: "Mr. Julius Zancig is a magician, a member of the Society of American Magicians of which I have been the President for the past seven years. I believe he is one of the greatest second-sight artists that magical history records. It would not be fair to disclose his methods despite the fact that Sir Arthur Conan Doyle put the stamp of genuineness on his work. Undoubtedly it *appeared* unfathomable to Sir Arthur and he therefore concluded that it was psychic and that there could be no other solution." Houdini's comments undoubtedly failed to shake Conan Doyle's conviction, for the author also believed that Houdini himself possessed psychic powers enabling him to perform his astonishing escapes and illusions — an idea strenuously rejected by the magician.

In any event, the question of the Zancigs was decisively resolved two years later when Julius Zancig, who was badly down on his luck, was forced to sell off the secret of his second-sight act — an ingenious verbal code — to a London newspaper.

The Man with the X-Ray Eyes

Unique among performing mentalists, Kuda Bux — "The Man with the X-Ray Eyes" — managed to excite the interest of psychic investigators without raising the ire of magicians. Born in Kashmir, India, in 1905, Bux first gained notoriety for walking across blazing coals or paraffin without suffering harm—a skill that he had mastered as a youth. By 1935, the stoical performer had been tested with a stroll across a fire measured at 1,400 degrees centigrade. However, after he emigrated to the United States in the late 1930s, Bux became better known for feats of so-called eyeless sight. His stage act raised simple blindfold effects to a level that may never be surpassed—or explained.

Bux disdained the use of plain cloth blindfolds. When he performed, he insisted that there be no possibility of "sneaking a peek." First, under the mentalist's instruction, audience members fastened large coins over each eyeball with adhesive tape. Then other spectators pushed masses of flour paste into both eye sockets, followed by cotton wads and more tape. Finally, they wound a wide surgical bandage around Bux's head. Not only did this lengthy process seemingly deprive the mentalist of his sight, but it added a drama to his appearance on stage. Bux asked only that no one plug up his nostrils, a stipulation that prompted one psychic researcher to ask, perfectly seriously, "Can anybody see with his nostrils?"

Even so encumbered, Bux was able to copy written messages, read books, and describe objects held up by the audience. On one occasion, he rode a bicycle through New York's Times Square in heavy traffic, an impressive feat even without the blindfold.

Bux delighted in misleading the press about the source and extent of his eyeless sight. Once, after dazzling a reporter with his various stunts while blindfolded, Bux made an elaborate show of looking for his glasses—without them, he explained, he was helpless. Similarly, Bux claimed: "If I am blindfolded, I don't make mistakes. But if I close my eyes I make the same mistakes as other people—I collide with objects." These statements delighted and bemused Bux's many magician friends, who would agree to play a game of cards with him only after they had laid down a strict rule: The mentalist was not permitted to wear his blindfold.

Many researchers and magicians were at a loss to explain Bux's abilities. The mystery deepened when, after a cataract operation damaged his vision, Bux continued to perform his act with the same clear-eyed results.

Perhaps the greatest tribute to Bux's skills came, quite unintentionally, from three female singers with whom he once made a tour of Britain. Assigned to a dressing room next door to Bux's, the women threatened to break their contract. The reason: "We would have no privacy. There is only one brick wall between us and Kuda Bux."

Horse Sense

In the 1920s, a psychic phenomenon of a very different kind captured the imagination of the public. Lady Wonder, the so-called educated mind-reading horse, was by no means the first animal to rise to psychic prominence. In

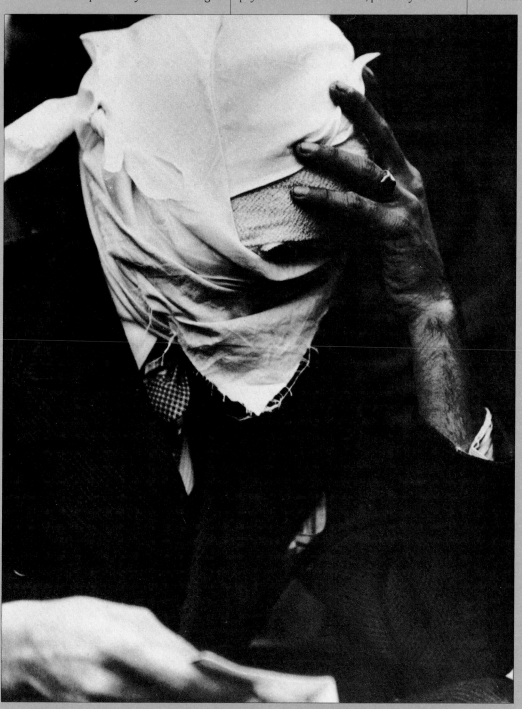

Although swathed beneath layers of gauze, tape, and sticky paste, Kashmiri mentalist Kuda Bux remained able to read books and to ride a bicycle, living up to his billing as "the Man with the X-Ray Eyes."

Lady Wonder's calling card (above) invites visitors to the horse's Virginia stable. For one dollar, the animal would answer questions using a keyboard (left).

1817, Toby, the Sapient Pig, startled Londoners by correctly indicating numbers and words thought of by his audiences. Geese, goats, seals, and even rats have all taken to the stage to perform seemingly telepathic acts. Yet Lady Wonder, whose stamping grounds were just outside Richmond, Virginia, was perhaps the first to warrant a full-scale psychic investigation.

The remarkable horse and her owner, Claudia Fonda, never traveled the show-business circuit. Instead, interested observers visited them at Lady Wonder's stable, where the animal stood poised behind an outsize typewriter, ready to peck out answers to questions by nudging the keys with her nose. For more than twenty-five years, Lady Wonder made headlines by predicting the outcomes of national elections, ball games, and—perhaps somewhat less surprisingly—horse races.

In 1927, the noted parapsychologist Joseph Banks Rhine went to Richmond to test the psychic horse. At first, Rhine found himself amazed by the horse's gifts. But after subjecting Lady Wonder to tests similar to those he applied to human subjects, he came to suspect that she was responding to subtle physical cues from her owner.

In separate tests that he conducted some years later, the magician Milbourne Christopher reached the same conclusion. According to Christopher, a luminary in the world of magic as both a performer and a historian,

the horse's predictions of future events could be chalked up to Mrs. Fonda's knowledge of current events and the propensity of the public to forget incorrect prophecies.

Lady Wonder herself remained quite unspooked by the controversy. As late as 1956, the horse continued to make—and predict—newspaper headlines.

Lady Wonder was only one among many mentalist performers to submit to psychic testing. In the 1930s, stage mentalists and average citizens alike came under the scrutiny of British mathematician Samuel George Soal in his quest to solve the mystery of mental telepathy. By 1939, Soal had conducted more than 120,000 tests on 140 people of varied background and education.

Mentalist under the Microscope

Easily the most unusual of Soal's subjects was a popular stage performer by the name of Frederick Marion. Born in Prague, Czechoslovakia, Marion was an adept entertainer who could locate hidden objects in a flash, even amid the most impenetrable clutter. The mentalist scored unusually well

Mentalist Frederick Marion holds his hand over face-down playing cards in a 1934 experiment. Marion was trying to probe the mind of Dr. S. G. Soal (left foreground) for the location of a preselected card.

in Soal's standard battery of ESP tests, but the researcher, familiar with the methods of other performers, had a suspicion that Marion was actually practicing noncontact thought reading. To test this theory, Soal built a heavy wooden device he called a sentry box for the psychic researchers to stand in during their experiments. The device restricted body movements, thereby limiting the physical signals that Soal and his assistants might unconsciously transmit to Marion. The box also shielded them from Marion's view while allowing the mentalist the voice and eye contact he required.

According to Soal, who published a report entitled *Preliminary Studies of a Vaudeville Telepathist*, Marion lost his ability to find hidden objects when his testers were shielded within the sentry box.

Still, such skills as muscle reading could not account for all of Marion's success, nor could the laboratory contain all of his feats. The performer frequently amazed his audiences with his ability to reconstruct past events from the lives of total strangers, based only on a half-dozen random words jotted on a slip of paper.

Marion related the story of how, during one such demonstration held at a large hall in London in 1934, a small, sharp-featured woman rose from the audience and accused the mentalist of employing confederates. She was Margot, Lady Oxford and Asquith, wife of the former prime minister of England. The mentalist quickly rose to the challenge. Inviting his critic to join him on stage, Marion asked Lady Asquith to concentrate on an important event from her past. Then he requested a random sample of her handwriting, which

S. G. Soal demonstrates his so-called sentry box, devised to limit the unconscious physical signals he could transmit to Marion. By adding or removing wooden panels, Soal controlled how much of his body the mentalist could see.

he had her seal away in a plain envelope.

Closing his eyes, Marion began to speak. "There is a large room," he said, "with bookshelves lining some of the walls. In this room, a man is sitting behind a huge table. A number of documents are spread on the table in front of him. He is reading something. He picks up a pen, then puts it down and rises from his seat to walk up and down the room. Returning to his seat, he once again picks up the pen. As he does so, a door behind him opens slightly. Somebody is looking into the room. The man writes, then takes a handkerchief from his pocket and dabs his eyes. He is crying."

Here a gasp from Lady Asquith halted the performer's narrative. Trembling, she turned to the audience and acknowledged that Marion had indeed read her private thoughts. She said: "The room Marion describes is the study of Number Ten Downing Street. The incident occurred there in August of 1914. At the moment Marion describes, my husband was in the act of signing the declaration of war against Germany."

Seeing Through the Iron Curtain

In 1910, a penniless eleven-year-old Polish boy boarded a train bound for Berlin, beginning a psychic career that would draw in such figures as Hitler, Stalin, Einstein, and Freud. As the grown psychic would later tell the story, the boy crouched under a seat that day in 1910, hoping to escape the notice of the ticket collector. When the conductor demanded to see his ticket, the boy, acting on a fearful impulse, handed him a worthless piece of paper torn from a newspaper.

"Our glances met," he later recounted, "and with all my strength I willed that he would take that piece of paper as a ticket."

Following a long pause, the conductor punched the piece of paper as he would an ordinary ticket and handed it back to the boy saying, "Why are you hiding under the seat if you have a perfectly good ticket?"

Wolf Messing claimed that this was his first experience of his remarkable powers of telepathic projection, or, in his words, the ability to cloud men's minds. It would be some time, however, before Messing learned to put his abilities to use. The performer later recounted how he wandered the streets of Berlin for days without food or shelter, finally succumbing to a cataleptic fit, the very condition that had plagued Washington Irving Bishop two decades earlier.

Fortunately, although Messing's body grew cold and stiff, the doctors who were

attending the stricken boy detected a faint heartbeat just as he was being dispatched to the morgue, thus sparing him the fate of his predecessor. His catalepsy brought him good fortune, however, in that it led to his first show-business job: lying motionless in a crystal casket at the Berlin waxworks, on display as a "living corpse."

By the age of sixteen, Messing had developed a mind-reading and so-called miracle-detective act in Berlin, in which he located valuables hidden among the audience. In this way, Messing came before two of the most famous, if amateur, psychic researchers of all time.

After a performance in Vienna, Messing recounted, he was invited to the apartment of thirty-six-year-old Albert Einstein. Ushering Messing into his study, Einstein introduced the teen-age entertainer to a visiting friend, Sigmund Freud, the founder of psychoanalysis. Freud insisted on testing Messing's mind-reading ability. The young Pole happily agreed to attempt a probe of the Viennese doctor's consciousness.

As Messing concentrated his energy, however, a look of consternation spread across his face. It was not that he could not fathom Freud's unspoken message, Messing said later; he simply could not believe it. Finally, with a shrug, the mentalist went to Einstein's bathroom cupboard and took out a pair of tweezers. Returning to Einstein, Messing hesitantly explained that Freud wished him to pluck three hairs from the physicist's mustache. Smiling, Einstein proffered his upper lip and, Messing later claimed, the mentalist carried out his task.

In the years that followed, Messing's reputation spread throughout the world. The thought reader performed in such places as Japan, Brazil, Switzerland, Italy, and India, where he claimed to have successfully read the thoughts of Mahatma Gandhi.

In Poland, Messing was able to find more work as a "miracle detective," placing his services at the disposal of the police force. One of the notable cases that Messing claimed to have solved involved a Count Czartoryski, a member of a wealthy and powerful Polish family. The theft of the Count's heirloom jewels had left the police baffled. As a last resort, the Count flew Messing to his castle in a private airplane.

The performer recounted how he probed the castle grounds with his mind, soon

Wolf Messing (opposite, right), whose prophesies were said to strike fear into Adolf Hitler, demonstrates his thought-reading act with an audience volunteer at a state university in Moscow.

coming to suspect the young son of one of the Count's servants. Inspecting the child's room, Messing found himself drawn to an enormous stuffed bear, which he snatched up and presented to the nobleman. When the bear was cut open, the missing jewels spilled forth, along with worthless bits of colored glass and other shiny objects. Evidently the boy had a fascination with glittering objects and hid any he came across inside the stuffing of his toy.

Overcome with gratitude, Count Czartoryski offered Messing a large reward. Messing refused, asking instead for a favor. The mentalist, who was Jewish, supposedly requested that the Count use his considerable political influence to help abolish a law infringing on the rights of Poland's Jews. The Count readily agreed, and within two weeks, Messing claimed, the law was repealed.

Messing was living in Poland when Hitler's army invaded in September of 1939. Two years earlier, before an audience of 1,000 people, Messing had predicted that Hitler would die if his armies turned east. Supposedly, news of the prophesy reached the führer, and he placed a price of 200,000 marks on Messing's head. As the German forces swept into the country, Messing fled.

The performer crossed into the Soviet Union hidden in a wagonload of hay. As a Jewish immigrant and practicing psychic, Messing's prospects in Stalin's Russia were poor. Yet, within three years, Messing rose to a position of prominence.

Messing's remarkable career in the Soviet Union began on a grim note in the city of Gomel. The mentalist later told how, in the midst of a sellout performance, two uniformed KGB officers stalked onto the stage, halted the proceedings, and dragged Messing off to a waiting car. After a long, anxious ride and a thorough search of his person, Messing found himself face to face with none other than Joseph Stalin.

The Soviet leader, apparently interested in Messing's gifts, invented a test of the mentalist's telepathic powers. Posing as an ordinary customer, Messing was to enter a Moscow bank and present the teller with a blank slip of paper. Then, by projecting his thoughts, Messing had to convince the teller to cash the blank slip as a check for 100,000 rubles.

The task, Messing asserted, went off without a hitch. He said that the elderly teller whom he approached looked at the blank slip (which had been torn out of an old school notebook), opened the bank's vault, and counted out the money. Later, when Messing returned the currency, the bewil-

dered teller examined the blank slip, looked at Messing in disbelief, and fell to the floor with a heart attack. "Luckily," Messing wrote, "it wasn't fatal."

Messing reported that, impressive as his demonstration was, it did not entirely satisfy Stalin, who proposed an even more difficult test. The Soviet leader owned a heavily guarded house in the country. If Messing had the ability to cloud men's minds, then surely he could slip past Stalin's secret police. Messing agreed to try.

The mentalist recounted that a few days afterward, as Stalin was working at his desk, he looked up to see Messing stroll casually through the door, having telepathically persuaded Stalin's guards that he was the head of the Soviet secret police. Stalin required no further tests.

Was Messing blessed with genuine psychic powers, or was he the most successful conjurer and self-promoter of modern history? Ludmila Svinka-Zielinski, a foreign correspondent who followed Messing's exploits, held that for the mentalist to have prospered under the constant scrutiny of the Soviet Union, he could not have dared fraud or even vain boasts. "To exist in the environment on such a level," she wrote, "Wolf Messing must be thoroughly authentic."

Messing himself waxed philosophical on the subject: "The time is coming," he once said, "when man will understand these phenomena. There is nothing strange, only what is not yet commonplace."

Radio's Mastermind

Even as Wolf Messing solidified his reputation behind the Iron Curtain, another colorful entertainer was stirring amazement in the United States. The son of poor German immigrants, Joseph Dunninger often claimed that his fate was sealed when, at the age of seven, he was taken to see a performance by Harry Kellar, one of the world's great magicians. Within a year, "Master Joseph Dunninger, Child Magician" had secured a booking at a Masonic lodge in New York. By the age of sixteen he was performing sleight-of-hand acts, and for the next ten years he seemed destined to pursue the career of a stage magician, without any particular emphasis on feats of mentalism.

In 1917, however, the twenty-five-year-old conjurer's career hit a turning point. To draw attention to the opening of his illusion show in Hartford, Connecticut, Dunninger staged a well-publicized blindfolded automobile drive through the city, on his way to tracking down an object hidden by a committee of townspeople. By updating the blindfolded carriage rides of Washington Irving Bishop, Dunninger scored one of the greatest publicity coups of his career. From that point on, he devoted himself almost exclusively to mentalism.

Two years later, Dunninger presented himself to a crowd of news reporters at the Boston Press Club as the president of an apocryphal organization called the American Psychical Society. In this capacity, Dunninger professed to have conducted important research into the science of telepathy. In the future, he claimed, every man and woman on earth would become skilled at mind reading, with incalculable benefits for the human race: Police would know the plans of criminals as soon as they were made, doctors would conduct psychic examinations of their patients, and communication by telephone would become obsolete.

In order to confirm his "purely scientific" discovery, Dunninger offered a demonstration of these powers. Distributing sheets of paper, the mentalist asked each reporter present to jot down a name, number, or other significant item. Then he asked them all to fold the slips and give them to a volunteer. Dunninger tucked these papers into an empty envelope, sealed it, and threw it on the floor, instructing his volunteer to hold it under his foot.

Without another glance at the envelope, Dunninger took a seat across the room and—to the astonishment of all present—promptly read off the contents of the paper slips.

Before long, the Boston newspapers were filled with accounts of this and other Dunninger marvels. One story told of how he singled one person out of a crowd of 3,000 at the Boston Common after a committee had sealed away a written description of the man. Another item told how Dunninger stunned the editors of a prominent newspaper by spelling out a headline they had secretly selected from their vast files. Before long, the "brilliant young investigator," as one newspaper called him, was prevailed upon to give a public demonstration of his gifts. Thus began a quarter of a century of top theatrical billing for the performer.

In presenting himself as a genuine psychic, rather than as a magician performing mind-reading tricks, Dunninger incurred a predictable wave of wrath from some of his former peers. One magician even drew up sketches that showed Dunninger palming

his audiences' slips of paper and reading them under the cover of a note pad. Dunninger denied the charge but revealed his ire by writing an article of his own that exposed the techniques of many other magicians. Eventually, the controversy led to Dunninger's expulsion from the National Conjuror's Association.

A promotional card emphasizes the dramatic appearance of Joseph Dunninger, who seemed to read minds over the airwaves.

By this time, however, Dunninger had become too successful to be damaged by a few accusations. Already a striking figure, the six-foot performer enhanced his dramatic image by growing out his thick black hair and sporting bright silk ties, a diamond stickpin, and white gloves and spats both on stage and off. He took his show across America, seeming to read the minds of contemporary notables such as Babe Ruth and Jack Dempsey. When not appearing in public, Dunninger commanded exorbitant fees at elite private functions given by such society figures as the Astors, the Tiffanys, and the Vanderbilts.

In 1943, the mentalist achieved even

greater celebrity with an enormously popular weekly radio program. At 6:30 on Sunday evenings, Dunninger's voice would be heard apparently reading the minds of the studio audience. He heightened his effects through the clever use of telephone hookups and remote studios, creating the impression that he could read minds at any distance.

In the 1950s, Dunninger moved to television, which proved an even richer environment for his talents. With the aid of remote cameras, he seemed to divine the thoughts of people in distant, inaccessible locations, including those of a naval officer aboard a submarine and a parachutist plummeting to earth.

Although he had a standing invitation from Joseph Rhine, the performer never submitted to formal testing by psychic researchers. His promotional literature, however, spoke of an early test by no less a scientist than Thomas Edison, who was quoted as saying, "Never have I witnessed anything as mystifying or seemingly impossible."

His detractors doubted such claims. As Dunninger's fame grew, so too did the attacks from professional magicians. "Dunninger," one conjurer said bitterly, "can't read the mind of a gnat. The only thing he can project is baloney." To all such charges, Dunninger had an unvaried response: If these magicians knew how his act was done, they were free to duplicate it. "The Dunninger act," he asserted proudly, "is the only thing in magic that has never been copied—if it is magic!"

"Close Your Eyes, Merv, and Concentrate"

Although Dunninger meant to discourage imitators by these words, a young man from New Jersey took the challenge seriously. As a child, George Kresge had been fascinated by the popular comic strip *Mandrake the Magician.* By the age of eleven, he took to the stage with a hypnosis act—although, as he later admitted, "I think more people fell asleep in the audience than on stage."

The lanky, bespectacled performer broke into television in the 1960s, using the title the Amazing Kreskin. Deeply influenced by Dunninger—he even adopted the elder performer's habit of doodling on a note pad while receiving psychic impressions—Kreskin also made good use of an effect patterned after that of another stage psychic, Franz J. Polgar.

The Hungarian-born Polgar, though nev-

At a Las Vegas casino, a relieved Kreskin plucks his paycheck from its hiding place in the seat lining of a car. The mentalist had promised to surrender the fee if psychic impulses failed to guide him to the check.

er as well known as Dunninger or Kreskin, had a dramatic flair that rivaled both. A consummate muscle reader, the short, gray-haired magician undertook in 1950 to locate a small silver money clip hidden on one of the 102 floors of the Empire State Building. Linked to a volunteer guide by a mere handkerchief, Polgar found the clip within a safe in the skyscraper's basement.

Later, he developed the effect that would fire the imagination of Kreskin. Before each performance, a committee would hide Polgar's paycheck somewhere in the theater, obliging the mentalist to find it psychically or forfeit his fee. Over the years, this test pressed Polgar to the very limits of his ability. Once, he discovered the check sealed inside a tennis ball. On another occasion, a Texas police chief slipped the rolled-up check into the barrel of his revolver.

In Kreskin's hands, the paycheck routine became the stuff of national drama. A fixture on television talk shows and later the star of his own program, the blindfolded Kreskin would take one end of a handkerchief held by a volunteer and frantically hunt through studio audiences in search of his check, darting to and fro until—usually just before a commercial break—he would fall upon the

Franz J. Polgar contemplates the Empire State Building as he prepares to find a money clip hidden inside. The Hungarian mentalist found the clip in a locksmith's subbasement office.

concealed check with a triumphant cry. The effect never failed to win applause and yield future bookings.

A friendly, engaging performer, Kreskin deftly sidestepped a large part of the controversy that had surrounded Dunninger by remaining vague about the source of his ability. Asked how he accomplished an especially dazzling mind-reading effect, Kreskin told an interviewer, "I would love to tell you how I do it, but I honestly don't know."

On another occasion, when he was asked whether he could lift a heavy object with the force of his brain waves, Kreskin was even more blunt: "No," he answered, "that would be magic."

A Simple Twist of Plate

Even as Kreskin chatted amiably on America's television screens, a young Israeli was preparing to take the scientific world by storm. In a few short years, Uri Geller, known as the psychic boy wonder, would skyrocket to global renown, leaving a trail of broken spoons, twisted keys, and quarreling scientists in his wake.

Born to a Hungarian family in 1946, Geller often claims that his psychic powers first manifested themselves after he received a severe electrical shock when he was five years old. By 1969, Geller began to exhibit feats of telepathy and psychokinesis in Israeli night clubs and on kibbutzim. Finding his talents underappreciated in his own country, where some critics accused him of fraud, Geller tried his luck in the United States.

Geller succeeded when the prestigious Stanford Research Institute, a scientific think tank in Menlo Park, California, included him in its ongoing psychic investigations. Although the results were sketchy and inconclusive, Geller's apparent abilities excited the investigators and conferred a legitimacy on the performer that made his name a household word.

The bulk of his fame came to rest on the

so-called Geller Effect—a display of psychokinetic strength in which the young Israeli appeared to break spoons in half, bend house keys, even halt cable cars in midair. But the entertainer also proved adept at displays of mind reading and thought projection. For one researcher, Geller duplicated a pencil sketch of a sailboat despite the artist's attempt to shield it from him. For another, he

Geller's nemesis, magician James Randi, has taken on Houdini's task of debunking psychic claims. He says most, if not all, psychics are only conjurers.

projected his own image onto photographic film seemingly by pressing his forehead against the capped lens of a camera.

In the early 1970s, it appeared that Geller had found the acceptance and respectability that had eluded his predecessors. However, he was not long on this pedestal. Like Bishop, the Zancigs, and Lady Wonder, Geller was to face his harshest criticism at the hands of a professional magician.

In 1973, Geller agreed to display his talents at the editorial offices of *Time*. Posing as a reporter, magician James Randi, a well-respected escape artist, observed Geller's effects at close quarters.

An accomplished mentalist in his own right, Randi took issue with Geller's claims. The endorsements that Geller had won from scientists meant nothing to the magician, who felt that scholars, believing themselves too smart to be fooled, were easily swayed by tricksters. When Geller completed his demonstration for the magazine's editors and left their offices, Randi promptly repeated every one of the young performer's effects.

To duplicate simple pencil sketches, Randi explained, Geller could have used a technique called pencil reading. Even if the person making the sketch held the pad out of sight, Geller would be able to recreate it by carefully tracking and then duplicating the movements of the artist's hand and pencil.

Similarly, Geller's celebrated key-warping feats were readily explained. Geller, said Randi, merely buckled the key against a tabletop.

Owing to Randi's influence, the magazine article that was subsequently published about Geller was considerably less flattering than it might otherwise have been. From that point forward, wherever Uri Geller went, James Randi seemed to follow close behind. When Geller appeared on one television show, Randi was there to supervise the conditions to preclude fraud. When Geller did mind-reading stunts, Randi improved on them. Although Geller's reputation in the United States has faded as a result, the Israeli mentalist maintains that Randi is merely a clever magician who has mimicked his results but not his methods. The effects are no less genuine, Geller says, for having been copied by trickery.

The two men seem likely to remain at odds for some time, the latest combatants in the struggle launched by Washington Irving Bishop a century ago. Perhaps the sagest words on the subject are those of Sydney and Lesley Piddington, an Australian thought-transference team popular in the 1950s. They ended their performances with a simple maxim: "Judge for yourselves."

Putting Psi to Work

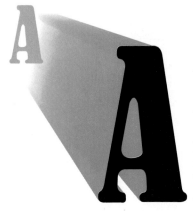

former carpenter from Canada, riding through Alexandria, Egypt, in 1979, suddenly exclaims: "We just drove over the top of Cleopatra's palace" — a structure that he describes in detail and locates for later excavation and exploration. A New Jersey housewife declares in 1967 that a missing boy is dead, and and describes where he will be found and how he is dressed; two months later, police confirm her prediction. A Missouri woman grips a sealed envelope and corroborates the commodities-market hunch it contains; after acting on the hunch, her client becomes a millionaire and buys her a house. In 1973, a retired police official in California describes a secret satellite-monitoring station 3,000 miles away in the state of Virginia in such detail that security officers launch an investigation to find the leak.

Some parapsychologists and others argue that such well-publicized incidents illustrate the potential rewards of applying supposed psychic gifts to humanity's endless quests for knowledge, justice, wealth, and power. Indeed, the possibilities can appear enormously attractive, not only to the psychics themselves and their individual beneficiaries, but to some of the largest, most conservative institutions of modern times—universities, corporations, and government agencies.

Partnerships of psychics and bureaucracies are uncomfortable at best. On one side is an organization dedicated to the reduction of risk, where decisions are made by committee and the most important ingredients of success are consensus and orthodoxy; on the other is an individual with a quirky talent whose performance is always uneven, and sometimes a bit theatrical as well. Yet a few large institutions continue to risk their reputations—if not their survival—by turning to psychics.

One field where psychic assistance seems especially appealing is archeology, a discipline that must build on clues that are widely scattered through space and time. To construct a picture of a society from a few shards of its pottery, a handful of broken spear points, or a sampling of cave drawings requires a creative imagination that almost borders on intuition. Small wonder that an archeologist may be tempted to leap beyond the bounds of the scientific method—as Frederick Bligh Bond did in 1908.

Bond, a thin, bespectacled, and intense man, had been given the job of excavating the sprawling ruins of the Benedictine Abbey of Saint Mary at Glastonbury, in southern England. The man and the job seemed perfectly matched. Bond was one of Britain's leading authorities on medieval church architecture; the Abbey of Glastonbury was an ancient pre-Christian ritual site where, it was said, Christianity had been introduced to Britain—and where the legendary King Arthur and Guinevere had supposedly been buried. Once a prosperous religious center populated by hundreds of monks (Ireland's Saint Patrick, among others) and thousands of workers, the abbey had been disbanded during the reign of Henry VIII in the sixteenth century.

Bond had been interested in Glastonbury for many years. The abbey was, after all, one of the most intriguing archeological puzzles of his time. He had also been interested in psychic phenomena since childhood. A longtime friend of Bond's, Captain John Bartlett, was an amateur psychic who had done some automatic writing—messages written by his hand that seemed to come from the spirit world.

One day in 1907, the year before Bond's Glastonbury appointment, he and Bartlett casually tried a cooperative experiment in automatic writing. Bond put his hand on Bartlett's and addressed his questions to any entity that might be present. His first: "Can you tell us anything about Glastonbury Abbey?" According to Bond, the answer was in the affirmative. During that and as many as a hundred subsequent sessions, he said later, spirits claiming to be long-dead monks, artisans, and workers communicated detailed descriptions and annotated drawings of the original abbey buildings. Among many other things, they indicated that there had once been a large chapel on the abbey's east side.

In his new job at Glastonbury, Bond soon found himself under pressure from both the church and a curious public to produce something interesting. He took a chance, started digging in the eastern section of the abbey, and discovered the chapel just where the automatically written floor plan said it would be. Now, relying entirely—but secretly—on his ethereal communicants, Bond went on to reconstruct several buildings: the refectory, the monks' dormitory, the cloisters, the chapter house, a pottery kiln, the monks' kitchen.

For years, Bond kept the alleged source of his professional inspirations a secret. Then, in 1918, he published a book, *The Gate of Remembrance,* in which he revealed the details of his conversations with the long-dead inhabitants of the abbey. Reactions were almost universally hostile. Embarrassed church officials first named a codirector to the restoration project, then appointed various supervisory committees, then slashed its budget. In 1922, they dismissed Bond and barred him from the abbey grounds. They stopped all excavation at the site and even filled in some of the existing digs.

Bond spent the rest of his life communicating with his company of departed monks, writing books about their alleged revelations to him, and trying to get back to work on the abbey. His latter efforts were stoutly and successfully resisted by the church, and in 1945, Bond died of a heart attack at the age of 82. The ruins of Glastonbury Abbey remain shrouded in the earth, with scores of architectural and historical details provided by Bond's unorthodox methods largely unchecked by modern researchers.

Bond is regarded as the first psychic archeologist, but he was far from the last. In 1935, a well-known Polish psychic named Stefan Ossowiecki was put to an odd test that would lead him deeply into investigations of the distant past. Born and raised in Moscow, Ossowiecki claimed to have discovered certain psychic abilities as a youth. He could see

colored auras flickering around people, he said, and could move small objects merely by concentrating on them. While he was interested in these abilities, they had not diverted him from a career as a chemical engineer.

In 1919, after narrowly escaping execution in the Russian Revolution, the forty-two-year-old Ossowiecki moved to Warsaw. There, his family fortune gone, he made a modest living as a chemical engineer and intensified his study and practice of extrasensory perception. His reputation as a clairvoyant grew. He helped find lost articles and missing people, and occasionally assisted in criminal investigations, but he never accepted money for applying his psychic gifts. He read everything he could find about parapsychology and readily volunteered to be the subject of psychic research projects.

The 1935 experiment had been created by a wealthy Hungarian named Dionizy Jonky, who had died eight years

Archeologist Frederick Bligh Bond (above) believed a monk named Johannes was among the spirits of Glastonbury Abbey who communed with him through automatic writing. Atop a fanciful sketched portrait, Bond directed to Johannes the question: "Is this like you?" The monk supposedly wrote this cryptic response: "I am as in a glass. Yes, I impelled the stylus. I be not as Apollus—but I be I — what matter? Thus I saw mine own [face] in clear pool o' mere. Johan."

earlier. As part of a large legacy, Jonky had provided for a test in psychometry, or object reading—the alleged ability to identify or tell something about an object by picking up thought waves supposedly implanted by someone previously associated with the article.

In his will, Jonky had devised a clever way to gauge a psychic's object-reading skills. He stipulated that eight years after his death a tiny, sealed package, its contents known only to him, be presented to a psychic adept at psychometry. In addition to testing that person's abilities, the results might also indicate whether the mental energy associated with the concealed object had dissipated after the owner's death.

In the presence of fifty witnesses, the package was placed in front of Ossowiecki along with fourteen photographs, one of them a picture of the long-dead Jonky. "I stilled my consciousness," said Ossowiecki later, "and moved to the realm of the superconscious."

Reviewing the photographs, Ossowiecki identified the picture of Jonky as the man who had prepared the package. After describing the dead man's life and interests and identifying the professor who had had custody of the package for the past eight years, the psychic turned to the package itself. "Volcanic minerals," he mused. "There is something here that pulls me to other worlds, to another planet." He was holding fragments of a meteorite, he said, adding that he also sensed sugar. The parcel was opened; it contained pieces of a meteorite, enfolded in a candy wrapper.

Later in 1935 came experiments in which Ossowiecki seemed to travel to prehistoric Egypt and Europe, observing people, events, and places with firsthand immediacy. He claimed that his surroundings, even his body, faded into the background when he was in such a so-called superconscious state, and that he was able to view history as if it were a film running in reverse. He said he could stop it, run it forward again, or change its perspective at will.

Those around him hardly knew what to make of his reports from the past; they needed an expert in prehistory to evaluate what Ossowiecki was seeing. And in March 1936, the psychic was introduced to Stanislaw Poniatowski, a fifty-two-year-old professor of ethnology at the University of Warsaw. It was a fateful meeting.

Poniatowski had long been interested in archeology. He wanted, as he put it, to find out "what links existed between the most primitive and uncivilized contemporary societies and their counterparts in the oldest prehistoric cultures." Moreover, he had been thinking about using psychics to probe the distant past and had worked out a rigorous procedure for such en-

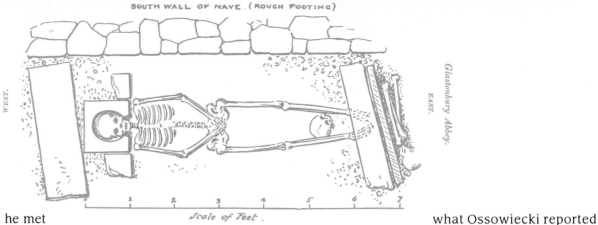

WEST.

EAST.

Glastonbury Abbey.

Scale of Feet.

Frederick Bligh Bond's dig at Glastonbury Abbey unearthed a skeleton with a skull between its ankles. Bond's dead spirits supposedly identified the remains: One enemy slew the other and, years later, was buried atop his victim.

deavors. So, when he met Ossowiecki, he knew that the time had come.

The psychic and the academician began a series of controlled experiments in psychometry. Poniatowski assembled a group of scientists from several disciplines—astronomy, mathematics, and geophysics as well as archeology—and asked them to submit detailed comments on what they observed during the session. Poniatowski would hand Ossowiecki an object to read and would guide the psychic's observations by asking questions. This last was a radical departure from usual procedure, in which the psychic was presented with a question and left undisturbed until the session was over.

When everything was ready, Ossowiecki was handed a flint tool. For about twenty minutes he said nothing while he put himself in the proper state of mind. The others in the room did as he had asked them; they chatted about other subjects and tried to avoid focusing their attention on him. At length Ossowiecki spoke: ''Thick, thick forest. Such a strange forest, black leaves, such dark color. Vast distances. Yonder there are places where there is no forest, clearings, and on them mushroom-like squat houses made of twigs smeared with clay. I see them well in this moment.''

For the next hour, he described in meticulous detail the people who he said had made the flint implement 10,000 years before—their appearance, customs, houses, and tools—until he complained of tiredness and a ''weight in the head.''

At regular intervals for the next three years, Ossowiecki took some object in hand and lofted himself into his special dimension, from which he reported in convincing detail on the lives of people who had lived as long ago as 300,000 years. In the main, what he described was consistent with what archeologists knew about these early societies. Of course, he went far beyond their general conjectures, and in many respects, what he claimed to see was unverifiable: the way two early humans copulated, for instance, or how a feather ornament was worn. It is claimed, however, that in many particulars

what Ossowiecki reported was not then known but was confirmed by much later research: the fact, for example, that prehistoric people used oil lamps. On the other hand, still later research contradicted many of his descriptions of early human appearance and culture.

By February of the year 1939, Ossowiecki had described and sketched eleven distinct prehistoric cultures. Poniatowski kept meticulous records—of the sessions, the artifacts used, and the comments offered by the committee of observers—for later verification. He even went so far as to attempt cross-checking Ossowiecki by employing another psychic but almost immediately gave up in disgust; this backup psychic could only give Poniatowski vague ramblings and broad guesses—which were based, he suspected, on the psychic's secret readings on the subject.

Then German forces invaded Poland and the years of brutal occupation began. Hitler ordered the extermination of ''the Jews, the intelligentsia, the clergy and the nobility of Poland.'' Yet neither Ossowiecki nor Poniatowski fled the country, as many other notables did. Ossowiecki worked day and night, making as many as thirty psychic readings a day for those who came to him inquiring about the fate of missing relatives and friends.

In 1941, while the Gestapo officials were busy dragging people from their homes for execution in the streets, the two time travelers resumed their work. Ossowiecki and Poniatowski were certain that they would be shot if discovered by the Germans. Nevertheless, they met regularly, compiling voluminous notes on eight more early cultures. Bowing to wartime conditions, Poniatowski gave up his plans for field excavations and began writing a book about the revelations.

But the fate so long deferred caught up with them at last. The Gestapo arrested Poniatowski in the fall of 1942 and detained him in prison until the war was almost over in 1945, at which time they shot him. By the time Poniatowski was killed, his friend and partner in psychic archeology was already

dead: In the fall of 1944, with the Russian and Allied armies pushing their way into Poland and Warsaw in open revolt, the Germans had rounded up nearly 10,000 Polish citizens, including Ossowiecki, herded them into a public park, and mowed them down with machine guns. ("I see that I shall die a terrible death," Ossowiecki had foretold not long before, adding "but I have had a wonderful life.")

In the years that followed Ossowiecki's gruesome death, other psychics continued to try their hands at archeology. However, more than two decades would elapse before another partnership between an academician and a psychic would produce notable results.

In the late 1960s, the distinguished Canadian educator J. Norman Emerson had watched with detached bemusement as his wife, Ann, began attending meetings of a study group interested in the work of the late psychic Edgar Cayce. Senior professor of anthropology at the University of Toronto, vice-president of the Canadian Archaeological Association, teacher of nearly ninety percent of Canada's professional archeologists, and a preeminent expert on Ontario's Iroquois Indian history, Emerson was, as he said later, "a hard-nosed researcher who had spent most of my adult life trying to apply the best scientific methods to my chosen field." His wife's growing interest in the arcane world of psychic affairs was "O.K. for a Wednesday evening meeting," he supposed, "but had nothing to do with me."

Despite any disinclinations, Emerson became friendly with Lottie and George McMullen, a couple that Ann Emerson had met at the Cayce group. George McMullen claimed to possess psychic abilities, but the educator was indifferent to them until Ann Emerson asked McMullen for advice about her husband's deteriorating health. McMullen responded, she recalled, "with great specificity and considerable authority. He said things he couldn't have known about Norm and made recommendations which a man with his grade-school education couldn't possibly have guessed."

Those recommendations made sense to Emerson. "Better yet," he said later, "they worked. When you are confronted with the prospect of an

Clairvoyant Stefan Ossowiecki, shown in this 1895 photograph as a cadet at St. Petersburg Technological Institute, often sketched what he saw in mental probes of the past. While psychometrizing a Stone Age tool, he drew a large-skulled creature he saw associated with it.

Psychics Search the Sea

If some psychics claim to be able to see across vast distances, why not beneath great depths? To explore that possibility, Stephan Schwartz, director of the Mobius Society, a Los Angeles parapsychology research group, devised the first undersea test of psychic archeology: Deep Quest.

In the spring of 1977, Schwartz mailed sets of four Pacific navigation charts to five volunteers. None was a professional psychic, but all claimed psychic powers. They were to use remote viewing to locate and describe shipwreck sites. Working independently, they picked several locations on the various maps. According to Schwartz, four of the five chose a single site on a chart showing some ten square miles of ocean near Santa Catalina Island. Be-

tween eighty-two and ninety-three years before, they said, a wooden sailing ship with a steam engine on board had suffered an explosion amidships and sunk at that very spot. Its remains would be found there at 277 feet.

In June, Schwartz and two of the psychics set out in a cabin cruiser to test the accuracy of the mental probes. Their equipment included the *Taurus I,* a thirty-two-foot-long submarine.

The evening before the first dive, one psychic reported new impressions. Among those she sketched were a ship's wheel, attached to a shaft, and a large stone block.

Three hours into his first dive, however, *Taurus* pilot Al Witcombe had seen nothing. His

sub could not get oriented on the sea bottom. Finally, a radio homing device was dropped into the target zone. Soon, *Taurus's* manipulator arm dug into the sand and extracted the first relic from the sunken ship.

Three days of diving yielded almost all the objects the psychics saw, including the ship's wheel and the strange stone slab. The distribution and type of charred wreckage suggested a wooden ship had exploded. Marine growth on the artifacts indicated they had been in place for decades. A federal marine-sites expert concluded that no known record could have cued the psychics to the shipwreck's location beforehand.

Submariner Al Witcombe views remains found by psychics.

extended, serious illness and then you try something and get well—it makes an impression. You respect the source no matter how crazy, imponderable or un-understandable it may be." The experience turned out to be the beginning of an unlikely but fruitful association.

George McMullen was a former carpenter and wilderness guide who proclaimed himself "an average guy." He was hesitant about using his apparent psychic gifts. Small wonder. Once, as a child, he had innocently—and accurately—predicted the death of a neighborhood boy in a motorcycle crash. His family and friends reacted with horror; his mother beat him, as if to drive out some demon, and the local minister accused him of having dealings with the devil.

For much of his later life, McMullen had kept his alleged powers to himself. But when, at the age of forty-nine, he found his gifts attracting the interest of a respected educator, he willingly responded.

Beginning in 1971, Emerson and McMullen conducted a series of object-reading sessions much like those held in Warsaw thirty years before. Emerson limited his inquiries to Iroquois history so that he would be able to evaluate McMullen's responses. In a typical early example, Emerson produced a tapered clay cylinder, apparently a fragment of a larger piece of unknown shape and function.

McMullen looked at it, felt it, and began to talk. First he told Emerson what the scholar already knew—where the fragment had been found and how old it was. Then he identified it as part of the stem of a ceremonial pipe, described exactly how it had been crafted, and sketched the entire pipe along with its decorations. Emerson immediately recognized the sketch as a typical pipe of that age and locale.

Many similar sessions followed, and for the next two years, McMullen roamed various Iroquois sites and relayed to Emerson what he sensed there. Explaining how he gathered his information, McMullen said he could hear people talking, sometimes so many at once that it was difficult to know which one to listen to. When someone asked him if they were dead people, the people said, according to McMullen: "Who is dead? You are the ones who are dead because you are so unaware."

As a result of this eavesdropping, according to Emerson, McMullen was able to "assess the age of the site, describe the people, their dress, their dwellings, economy and general behaviour" with eighty percent accuracy.

Convinced that McMullen's psychic abilities were real and that the information they produced was useful, Emerson resolved to share this new source of knowledge. He did so at the March 1973 annual meeting of the Canadian Archaeological Association.

Coming from the man known as the father of Canadian archeology, it was a stunning declaration: "It is my conviction that I have received knowledge about archaeological artifacts and archaeological sites from a psychic informant who relates this information to me without any evidence of the conscious use of reasoning." He concluded that "by means of the intuitive and parapsychological a whole new vista of man and his past stands ready to be grasped."

Emerson's colleagues were shocked and skeptical. But given the credentials of the speaker, they were interested. That evening, one of their number asked for a demonstration. He produced a crude carving of a human head in black stone, confiding to Emerson that it had been found in an Indian site on the Queen Charlotte Islands off the coast of British Columbia, Canada's westernmost province. However, McMullen, who had accompanied Emerson to the meeting, declared that it had been carved by a black African from Port-au-Prince in the Caribbean who had been taken to the west coast of Canada as a slave.

Emerson, having just staked his reputation on a man who was now speaking nonsense, was mortified. As far as he or anyone else knew, no blacks had lived in British Columbia before modern times. The embarrassed Emerson borrowed the carving and had McMullen read it again later. He even tried other psychics but claimed that he always got the same account of its African creator. Then a colleague supplied some support. One of his former students, involved in cataloguing an extensive museum collection of West African art, was shown the enigmatic head and told nothing of its background. Without hesitation, he identified the piece as African in motif.

Finally, two years later, anthropologists conducting an unrelated blood analysis of Indians in British Columbia found definite evidence in one tribe of a Negro ancestor.

Emerson died in 1978, but McMullen continued to assist other archeologists with their projects, in Canada as well as in other countries. It was while he was on an expedition to Alexandria, Egypt, in 1979 that he informed his companions that they had just driven over the long-buried remains of the queen Cleopatra's palace.

"See the lighthouse out there?" he asked, while the others looked out at an empty sea. Excitedly, McMullen told of a grand palace with white columns and marble statues that spread from the city out into the water. He even described large glass beads on the floor of the palace—all of which divers and archeologists later validated by exploration of a structure that had stood there more than 1,000 years ago.

To be sure, the revelations of psychic archeology have not gone unchallenged by skeptics. Frederick Bligh Bond is said to have had abundant visual and historical clues for his finds at Glastonbury Abbey; he was, after all, an expert on medieval churches. And as American archeologist Marshall McKusick has pointed out, the spirits consulted by Bond did not communicate in the idioms of their own day, but in "modern English larded with anachronisms, and such verbal awkwardisms and archaic words as were fashionable among nineteenth-century poets." (Bond supporters, of course, could argue that ghosts capable of surviving over many centuries would presumably have within their powers the ability to

Clairvoyant Gerard Croiset points to where in Holland's
Vliet Canal, he foresaw, the body of six-year-old Wimpje Slee would be found.
Croiset's prediction in the 1963 case proved correct.

126

The theatrical clairvoyant Peter Hurkos claims his psychic revelations are 87.5 percent accurate. Critics accuse him of ambiguity and of misrepresenting his failures.

speak in any fashion they might choose.) As for Stefan Ossowiecki, much of the original documentation for his work was destroyed during World War II, and critics have observed that a large part of his psychic archeology seemed to be based on misconceptions current in the late 1930s. The unlettered George McMullen's performances in Egypt and other Middle Eastern countries may be difficult to explain fully on the basis of prior knowledge or interest, but his readings of Canadian Indian artifacts might well have stemmed from his exposures to Indian cultures when he was a wilderness guide. Indeed, McMullen himself has balked at being called a psychic: "I hate that word. To me, you link those with mediums and fortune-tellers. I don't do those things. I'm an intuitive."

Whatever its practitioners might be, psychic archeology continues to fascinate. One enthusiast has been moved to propose that the archeological team of tomorrow may include "biofeedback technicians, a staff parapsychologist, and of course, a team of psychics"—all using methods "whose sophistication will be as incomprehensible to us as the world of electricity was to nineteenth-century man."

While there is great academic interest in the distant past, the demand to know what has happened more recently is often far more urgent—to police departments, for example, or to the families of missing or murdered people. Public pressure and private desire for results can become so extreme that stymied detectives often seek out the services of psychics despite the potential for embarrassment.

Any number of supposed psychics have stepped forward, or have been recruited, to help investigate crimes, but

the two best-known extrasensory detectives of the twentieth century have been Gerard Croiset and Peter Hurkos. Both were born in the Netherlands, just two years apart, and had early premonitions of later psychic talents. Apparently, they met only once, and their careers were quite different.

Croiset, born in 1909, had a turbulent childhood. Often deserted by his natural father, and for a time abandoned by his mother, the young Gerard was raised in a succession of foster homes, including one in which the favored form of discipline was to chain the boy to a stake in the floor. He was often hungry for food, and always starved for affection.

As a young man, Croiset had been unable to hold even menial jobs and had failed as a grocer. But in the late 1930s, he began to gain a reputation as a psychic who had an uncanny ability to peer into both past and future by way of psychometry. He made an uncertain living as a clairvoyant throughout the German occupation of Holland, during which he was twice arrested and released by the Gestapo.

In 1945, the moderately well-known but aimless Croiset met Willem Tenhaeff, an unpaid lecturer in parapsychology at the University of Utrecht. Tenhaeff was an enthusiastic researcher into the abilities of apparent psychics, and Croiset was willing to be studied: "I decided that the best use I could make of my empty life," he said later, "was to do all these scientific tests that Professor Tenhaeff wanted."

Tenhaeff put Croiset through a series of psychiatric and psychic examinations at the university. The professor had analyzed dozens of psychics—whom he termed *paragnosts,* a word meaning "beyond knowledge"—during a period of twenty years, but he pronounced Croiset the most gifted of

Psychic Crime Fighters

Clairvoyants often seem stymied by high-profile crimes, but they have helped police in less-publicized cases. When a seven-year-old Los Angeles boy disappeared in 1978, for example, investigators called in a psychic whose legal name was simply Joan. She said the boy had been murdered, and she described the killer. Joan thought the resulting police sketch not quite true to her vision, but the missing boy's father identified it immediately. The suspect, a family acquaintance, was eventually convicted of murder.

In another California case, in 1981, Mountain View police asked psychic Kay Rhea to help identify a woman whose skull was found in a city dump. A police artist sketched Rhea's impressions. Independent of that effort, a forensic anthropologist made a plaster cast of the skull. It matched the sketch remarkably. Pictures of both appeared in newspapers, but the victim was never identified.

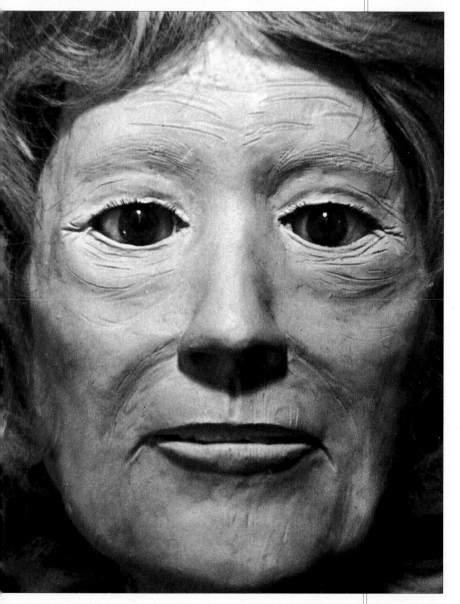

Psychic Kay Rhea's description resulted in a police sketch of a decapitation victim whose skull had been discovered in a city dump in Mountain View, California (opposite page). The sketch bears a marked resemblance to an anthropologist's plaster reconstruction of the skull (below). Both renditions were widely circulated, but the victim remains unidentified.

them all. For the next two decades and more, Tenhaeff would spend much of his time studying and promoting Croiset's abilities. During this time, Croiset's fame became national, then international; and Tenhaeff became the world's first professor of parapsychology and the director of the University of Utrecht's pioneering Parapsychology Institute.

With increasing frequency, police departments in the Netherlands, other European nations, and eventually even the United States and China asked Croiset, through Tenhaeff, to assist in particularly perplexing cases. Few of these cases could be hailed as triumphs of psychic crime solving, yet some of them have remarkable elements nevertheless. In 1961, for example, four-year-old Edith Kiecorius of Brooklyn, New York, had disappeared on the afternoon of February 22; when she had not been found three days later, police were assuming the worst. Public interest in the case was intense, and on February 25, an official of KLM, the Dutch airline, located Croiset and offered to fly the psychic to New York if he would help solve the mystery of Edith's disappearance. "I have never been to New York," said Croiset. "If I go there now, I would choke on all the impressions and would not be able to see a thing." Instead, he asked that further information, a photograph of the child, a map of New York, and an item of her clothing be flown to him in Holland.

But before hanging up, Croiset began to talk about the case. The child was dead, he declared, and he described in general terms the location of the body (a tall building with a billboard on top, near an elevated railroad and a river) and the man who murdered her (small, fifty-four or fifty-five years of age, south European, sharp-faced, wearing gray). The next day Croiset went over the materials flown from New York and refined his descriptions. The building in which the body lay "has, I think, five floors. On the second floor I get a strong emotion. The man I described yesterday is a little older, between fifty-four and fifty-eight years of age. He has a small, sharp, tawny face."

About six hours later, as part of a general search unconnected with Croiset's clues, police broke into a second-story room in a gray building near an elevated railroad and the Hudson River—and found the child's body. The landlord identified the renter of the room, who was soon arrested and convicted of the crime. He was small, sharp-nosed, and swarthy, and

Representing one of Gerard Croiset's psychic failures, this hole in a suburban backyard turned out not to be the grave of Judge Joseph Force Crater. Crater's celebrated disappearance in 1930 made news again in 1959 when Croiset claimed the prominent judge had been murdered at a house in Yonkers, New York, and buried behind it. The story squared with old clues involving the house, which had been owned by one of Crater's political cronies. However, when the backyard was excavated, no remains were found. Crater's fate is still unknown. Here the home's 1959 owner peers into the empty "grave,"

dressed predominantly in gray checks. There were discrepancies, to be sure: The building was four, not five, stories in height; there was no billboard; the culprit was from England, not south Europe. And while Croiset had been more often right than wrong in what he said about the case, the police had solved it without his help, and his role was not mentioned at the time. A number of critics have pointed out that many of Croiset's alleged contributions to crime solving were grossly exaggerated by his mentor, Tenhaeff. In one notable example, the Dutch investigator Piet Hein Hoebens found that facts about an attempted murder case, reputedly perceived psychically by Croiset, had in fact been published in Dutch newspapers five days earlier. But Croiset's reputation continued to grow—thanks largely, perhaps, to the fact that English-speaking commentators, unable to read Dutch, relied on the enthusiastic Tenhaeff for their information.

This lack of clear-cut results is characteristic of psychic detective work. Indeed, however accurate and valuable the clues provided by a psychic may be, they cannot be presented in a court as evidence, and no police officer will make an arrest or declare a case solved solely on the basis of such advice. The usual official response is to listen and wait, and when the case is resolved, the contribution of the psychic may be almost impossible to divine.

Sometimes, it seems, a psychic may even lead police astray, as apparently happened when Croiset's fellow Dutchman and psychic Peter Hurkos became involved in a celebrated American murder case in 1964. After nineteen-year-old Mary Sullivan became the eleventh victim of the notorious Boston Strangler that year, Massachusetts Attorney General Edward W. Brooke appointed a special state investigative team to work together with the Boston police. And, willing to do anything in order to stop the killing and catch the strangler, he called in Peter Hurkos.

Hurkos's career as a psychic had begun in 1941, when the thirty-year-old laborer had fallen four stories from a building he had been painting in The Hague. Taken unconscious to a hospital, he was diagnosed as having a brain concussion and possibly severe neurological damage. When he regained consciousness four days later, he had amnesia, but when he heard his wife's voice, he cried, "Bea, what are you doing here? Where's Benny? The whole room is burning with Benny." Five days later their son Benny was trapped in a fire, and was rescued just in time from a burning room.

Hurkos never recovered his full mental faculties after the accident; he remained unable to concentrate long enough to do ordinary work or even read a book. But he began to demonstrate apparent psychic abilities and soon began to use them in theatrical presentations. He was far more visible and self-promoting than Croiset, and seldom consented to the supervision of researchers such as Tenhaeff.

According to Hurkos, he was asked in 1947, soon after launching his show-business career, to help with an unsolved murder of a young coal miner in the Dutch province of Limburg. Hurkos reportedly fingered the victim's coat, then told police that the miner's stepfather had done the shooting. The murder weapon, he said, was on the roof of the dead man's house; police found the gun and obtained fingerprints from it that led to the stepfather's conviction.

In 1948, after Hurkos had become famous in Europe as the man with "radar eyes" and an "X-ray brain," he moved to the United States. There, with his thick Dutch accent and flamboyant ways, he became as well known in America as he had been in Europe. If his successes were modest, his publicity was voluminous; he received credit for cases he did not solve and blame for failures in cases to which others thought he had made useful contributions. The Boston Strangler case was perhaps typical.

By that time Hurkos was living in Hollywood, California, where he was doing a lucrative business as a psychic adviser to various movie stars, including Marlon Brando and Glenn Ford. He agreed to work on the Boston Strangler case with some reluctance, because he found criminal cases, especially violent ones, highly disturbing.

Aware that public knowledge of their foray into psychic sleuthing might cause an outcry, the special investigative team registered Hurkos under a false name in a suburban Boston motel. On January 30, 1964, the investigators brought

130

in two large boxes of objects for Hurkos to psychometrize. These items included nylon stockings and scarves that the Strangler had used to kill his victims, along with nearly 300 police photos taken at the crime scenes.

For the next six days, Hurkos immersed himself in the case. He ran his fingers over the backs of the photographs, and without looking at them, described the circumstances of the murders depicted and the identities and backgrounds of the victims. He angrily discarded one picture, unconnected to the case, that had been included as a test. He kept at it for eighteen hours a day, and at night often slept with an item of clothing from one of the murdered women. Then one day, grasping a small comb that had belonged to a victim, he ran it across a map of Boston. Stopping at Boston College, he exclaimed: "Here you find the killer."

Police later showed him a letter written to the Boston College School of Nursing by a man who rambled on about wanting to interview a typical nurse for a possible magazine article and eventual matrimony. Hurkos held the letter, then excitedly announced that its writer was the Strangler—a homosexual woman-hater, about fifty-two years old, who spoke with a French accent and had thin, receding hair, a pointed nose, and a prominent Adam's apple.

Hurkos said he began to dream about the murderer. "I hear two voices," he explained, "my normal voice and his high voice, and then I was fighting mad." He said the killer, a former monk, slept "on a cot, on springs, without mattress" in a room "like a junk pile." The man took showers with his shoes on, said Hurkos, and he kept a diary that would prove his identity as the Boston Strangler.

Hurkos's description eventually led police to the apartment of a man they referred to as Thomas P. O'Brien—his real name was withheld. The man, his surroundings, background, and habits answered Hurkos's description in virtually every aspect. Lacking tangible evidence for a murder warrant, investigators instead managed to get the man temporarily committed to a mental hospital for observation. He responded by voluntarily committing himself indefinitely, a move that also made it legally impossible to try him for murder.

Months later, a maintenance man named Albert De-Salvo was arrested for a series of rapes, diagnosed to be a schizophrenic, and committed to the same mental institution that was treating the man called O'Brien. DeSalvo soon boastfully confessed to the eleven Boston Strangler killings, plus two more, and provided enough detail about the individual cases to convince the police that he was telling the truth. Ironically, DeSalvo was beyond prosecution—having been declared insane—and the case of the Boston Strangler was closed without a conviction or even a trial.

His perceived failure in the Boston Strangler case—a failure he never admitted, always insisting that he had identified the real Strangler—discredited Hurkos for a time. His seeming knowledge of the crimes derived from photographs he never looked at, and his description of the bizarre ''O'Brien'' derived from dreams, were obscured by the equivocal outcome of the case. Indeed, it seems that well-publicized crime cases have never been fruitful for alleged psychics.

Several were called in when Patricia Hearst, daughter of newspaper magnate Randolph Hearst, was kidnapped in 1975. The first was an energetic New Jersey housewife named Dorothy Allison. Once again, the results were indeterminate. Although Allison could not tell exactly where the missing girl was, she was credited on several occasions with advising authorities correctly about Hearst's general location and the nature of her activities.

Like many of her colleagues, Allison had done far better on more obscure cases. She had first become known as a psychic after she announced in December of 1967 that she had dreamed about the fate of a missing New Jersey boy, five-year-old Michael Kurcsics. Michael was dead, she said, and his body was caught in the drainpipe of a pond; his shoes were on the wrong feet, and he wore a green snowsuit with a religious medal pinned to it. In the background, she saw a gray wall, a building with gold lettering, and the number eight.

Two months later, the boy's body was discovered in a

The Search for a Missing Girl

Dorothy Allison focuses on the missing Debbie Kline's class ring. Allison says she has been clairvoyant since childhood and believes she inherited the power from her mother.

In December of 1976, a desperate letter made its way to the New Jersey home of Dorothy Allison. ''Please help me if you can,'' it begged. ''I don't know what else we can do.'' The writer was Jane Kline of Waynesboro, Pennsylvania. Her daughter, Deborah Sue Kline, had been missing for almost five months.

The pretty, eighteen-year-old hospital worker, recently graduated from high school, had left her new job on a warm July evening and had not been seen since.

Months of police work had yielded no trace of the girl. As Christmas neared, her parents hung Debbie's stocking on their mantle—a forlorn hope. The Klines were near despair. Then Jane Kline read in a tabloid about Dorothy Allison, a supposedly psychic housewife who specialized in finding missing children.

Allison telephoned the Klines after receiving their letter. At the Kline home the night of the call was a newspaper photographer, Kenneth Peiffer. Along with reporter Robert Cox, Peiffer had been covering the case for the local newspaper, the Record Herald. Jane Kline was happy to hear that Allison planned to come to Waynesboro soon but warned that her family would not be able to pay much.

''Now you listen to me,'' Allison said. ''Your money is no good. I don't want it. I won't take it.'' Then she asked to talk to Peiffer. Skeptical of all psychics, the photographer felt what he later described as ''an unmistakable sensation of charged energy'' as he listened to Allison give particulars about the case.

''I see two people involved,'' she said. ''Their names are Ronald and Robert or Richard, I'm not sure of the second one. [She would later settle on Richard.] I see one of their last names as having double letters in it.'' She said a hill and a line would somehow figure in the case. In a call to Peiffer several days later, she sounded a tragic note. ''Debbie is dead,'' the psychic said. ''I know that. When I come down there, we will be looking for a body.''

The search began when Allison arrived in Waynesboro on January 22. Accompanied by Cox, Peiffer, and a state trooper, the psychic toured the area where Debbie had lived and had more psychic pictures. She mentioned several times that fire was important to one of the abductors. Both men had run afoul of the law often, she said, and both were already in jail on other charges. Both were rapists. Both had double letters in their names. The victim's body would be found on a hill's summit and would be ''not completely buried—not deep.'' Allison said she envisioned something about the color yellow, a dump, a shoe, a plastic swimming pool All would be important.

Then she made another prediction—

drainpipe in Clifton, New Jersey. He was wearing a green snowsuit, and when police removed his rubber boots, they found that his sneakers were on the wrong feet. Nearby were a gray concrete building, a factory with gold lettering on the front door, and an elementary school—P.S. 8.

Allison's association with the Hearst case may not have been a resounding success, but it was almost a triumph compared to her work on another famous case five years later. In 1980, Atlanta police were unable to solve a series of brutal murders of young blacks, and were increasingly desperate as the case took on racial overtones and national celebrity. They received some 1,300 offers of help from self-styled psychic detectives and eventually decided to consult Allison, among others. Afterward, an Atlanta police officer described Allison as "that wacko broad" who had come up with forty-two possible names for the murderer—but not the correct one.

Such failures tend to discredit psychic crime solvers, despite the fact that they themselves seldom claim a high success rate. One, the appropriately named John Catchings, concedes that only one in five of the clues he provides is completely correct—and that he is able to be of help in little more than half the cases he takes on. Dorothy Allison says she has worked on 4,000 cases but claims credit in only seventy-six of them.

Few cases displayed the supposed strengths and obvious weaknesses of psychic police work more starkly than did that of the Yorkshire Ripper. Over a five-year period beginning in 1975, thirteen women were violently murdered in northern England. The slayer, dubbed the Yorkshire Ripper, would kill two or three women within a period of several days, slashing their bodies and crushing their skulls with hammers. Then he would disappear for months.

During the long hunt for the killer, the police received far more psychic help than they could use. One clairaudient named Doris Stokes listened to a tape recording reportedly made by the killer and came up with a description of sorts: He was five feet eight inches tall, his name was Ronnie or Johnnie,

an odd one, since there were no new leads in the six-month-old case. They were about to solve it, she said. One suspect would confess and implicate another.

In fact, police had gotten several breaks in the case about the time Allison entered it. Stories from three informants led them to a man already in custody on an unrelated charge. His name was Richard Lee Dodson. Owner of a long police record, Dodson had once been awaiting sentencing on a rape conviction when his home burned down, killing his wife and three children. He escaped unhurt. On January 26, Dodson confessed and named Ronald Henninger as his accomplice in the murder of Debbie Kline. Henninger's rap sheet included rape and manslaughter.

Dodson led police to the body. They traveled up a mountain road marked by highway signs warning of the steep grade. The signs were bright yellow. The snowy top of Fannettsburg Mountain, 150 feet from a county line, was a dump site. There a trooper saw a shoe protruding from the snow. When the snow was removed, Debbie Kline's body lay half-buried beneath debris. It was partly covered by a blue plastic swimming pool.

Police and coroners view the body of Debbie Kline, found half-buried in a mountaintop dump in rural Pennsylvania. Following Dorothy Allison's clues, two reporters were only minutes behind police in locating the body.

his last name started with an *M* and he lived in Tyneside or Wearside. He had, she said, a "scar below his left eye which twitches when he gets agitated." She also reported a telepathic conversation with the Ripper's mother, who said her son was separated from his wife.

Gerard Croiset joined the quest, too. When he envisioned the Ripper, the renowned Dutch psychic agreed with Stokes's characterization, adding that the killer had long hair cut straight across the neck, limped because of an injured knee, and lived in the heart of Sunderland. Other psychics contributed additional details over the years: The Ripper was a man of average build with dark hair; he wore a black duffel coat bearing the white letters *RN;* he lived in Barnsley or Sheffield; he was a washing-machine mechanic; he sometimes disguised himself as a woman.

As it turned out, virtually every one of these particulars was wrong. Included among the mistakes was the claim by one Nella Jones, from Kent, that the killer was a transvestite. Jones was much closer to the mark in other areas, however. In a series of predictions given to journalists between October 1979 and January 1980, she said that the Ripper's name was Peter, that he was a truck driver working for a company whose name began with the letter *C,* and that he lived at No. 6 on a street in Bradford, Yorkshire. When the killer was tracked down in January 1980, he turned out to be Peter Sutcliffe, a truck driver for a company called Clark Transport, who lived at No. 6 Garden Lane in Bradford.

The mixed results, the lack of evidence that will stand up in court, and the lurid publicity are all powerful arguments against police department use of psychics. Indeed, few law enforcement officials care to admit that they consult these unconventional sleuths, and a 1979 study conducted by the *Journal of Police Science and Administration* at the Los Angeles Police Department concluded that psychics had not provided significant additional information leading to the solution of any major crimes.

Despite all these problems, one thing is certain: The next time a police department faces increasing pressure to solve an especially notorious crime, it will receive advice from psychic counselors. Some of the guidance will be useless, and some of it will be surprisingly accurate. All the police will have to do is figure out which is which.

If psychic information about the past can yield knowledge or justice, a sense of the future could lead to something many people desire even more passionately—money. And psychics are sometimes consulted not only by individuals looking for a tip on the stock market or a secret route to wealth, but by giant corporations deciding where to drill an oil well or whom to appoint as a top executive.

In fact, links between extrasensory perception and the hard-nosed, no-nonsense business world are being recognized with increasing frequency. Many executives believe there is more to their decision making than logic and calculation. As Alfred P. Sloan, one of the towering figures in the history of General Motors, once put it: "The final act of business judgment is intuitive."

For instance, the founder of Budget Rent-a-Car, William Sechrist, has said he sometimes makes use of a sixth sense in business. He recalled that in the early days of his enterprise he once came across a rental contract, in a stack of others, that just did not seem right. He checked on it, and discovered that the customer had written a bad check and had provided bogus telephone numbers. He immediately ordered the rental car re-

Sunday People

JULY 1, 1979   No. 5083 16p   ★   U

What woman psychic 'saw' for The People

FACE OF THE RIPPER

FAMOUS clairvoyant Doris Stokes has "seen" the face of the Ripper.

The Ripper — as Doris Stokes "saw" him for the Sunday People.

trieved. On another occasion, he dreamed that a key employee at a distant office was not working as he should have been; on checking the next day, Sechrist confirmed that the man had taken the previous day off to move and someone else had punched the time clock for him.

There are indications that Sechrist's experiences are far from unusual. A ten-year study completed in the 1970s concluded that a high proportion of successful executives believe in some kind of extrasensory perception. The research, conducted by John Mihalasky and Douglas Dean at the Newark College of Engineering in New Jersey, also concluded that the strong, dynamic, get-things-done sort of executive scored consistently higher in tests of ESP abilities than did the more easygoing type. As a result of this and other studies, the two researchers advised corporations to include testing people for extrasensory abilities in their executive-selection process.

Newspapers ballyhooed alleged psychic contributions to the Yorkshire Ripper case. A Sunday People sketch (left) inspired by a clairaudient in no way resembled the real Ripper. The Daily Star's so-called psychic drawings of alleged Ripper intimates were equally off base.

Such studies of how ESP has been used in business in the past offer no help in predicting the value of a current hunch or precognition. If supposedly psychic insights can be neither dismissed as completely useless nor accepted as infallible, what may be needed is a rational technique for dealing with a welter of predictions.

Perhaps the best such system now available was developed shortly after World War II when the Air Force retained the Rand Corporation, a prestigious research organization, to predict the number of atomic bombs that an enemy would need to deploy in order to cripple the United States. When the work of Rand mathematicians Olaf Helmer and Norman Dalkey was declassified years later, researchers were less interested in the answer they came up with (150 to 400 bombs) than in the technique they used, which was later employed to solve civilian problems as well.

They called it the Delphi method, after the legendary Greek oracle at the temple to Apollo at Delphi. The procedure was to ask a large number of experts to make individual projections in response to a question. (An example: What will be the total payroll of the automobile industry in a certain future year?) Later the forecasters were shown their colleagues' work and asked to refine their own predictions. The consensus that emerged after several such rounds was found to be significantly more accurate than any individual forecast. In

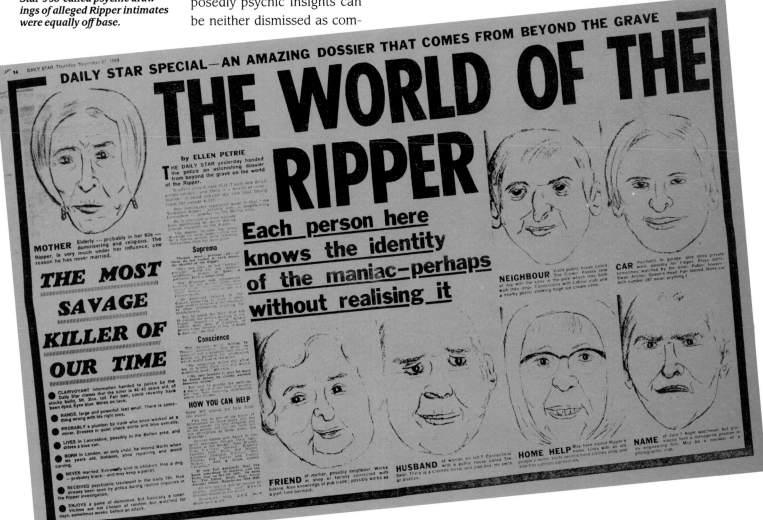

the case of the auto industry payroll, the Delphi prediction was within eight percent of the actual figure.

Enthusiasts have suggested that the Delphi method seems to work so well because it makes full use of both sides of the brain. Recent research indicates that the brain has two largely independent hemispheres of activity: a left side that deals in logical analysis and a right side that works through intuition. According to this view, the initial Delphi forecast draws on the respondent's intuitive right brain, and the later analysis and revision make use of left-brain abilities.

However it works, the Delphi method has become one of the most widely used of modern forecasting techniques, and is applied regularly by large corporations and government agencies. While it cannot be regarded as a truly psychic procedure, it does represent a large-scale effort to incorporate elements of intuition, precognition, and extrasensory perception into American business.

Individual psychics, meanwhile, have had more spectacular involvements with big business. One such association began when a young Missouri woman named Beverly Jaegers, who had gained some renown as a psychic detective, was asked to take on a different kind of assignment. In December of 1974, commodities broker John Peters Dixon presented her with a sealed envelope, as she had instructed him to do. Inside was a question about a tantalizing dream. As Jaegers later told the story, she ran her hands over the envelope and soon saw "a tree, covered with reddish-colored berries." Dark-skinned people in big hats were picking the fruit, but their large baskets contained only a sprinkling of shriveled berries. Dixon was ecstatic. He had dreamed that London coffee futures would rise to £2,900 from their then-current, long-time level of £600. As far as he was concerned, Jaegers had confirmed his hunch.

Dixon scraped together all the money he could and invested it in coffee futures; not long afterward, a sudden freeze in Brazil and political unrest in Angola caused the world sup-

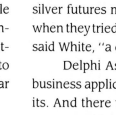

ply of coffee to dwindle. Two years later, Dixon was a millionaire, and out of gratitude he bought Jaegers a $60,000 house.

The success brought Jaegers a great deal of fame—and much mail asking her to guess whether individual stocks would go up or down. Her method was simple. She advised clients to place the name of a stock or commodity on a piece of paper, fold the paper, and place it in a sealed envelope. Jaegers would then hold the envelope. "If it's a good stock," she explained, "the envelope feels hot."

In 1982, the *St. Louis Business Journal* pitted Jaegers against nineteen stockbrokers who were asked to select five stocks that they expected to gain in value during the following six months. When the time was up, the Dow Jones Industrial Average—the widely used barometer of stock market trends—had fallen by eight percent. The portfolios selected by sixteen of the brokers had lost value. The stocks that had been picked by Jaegers, on the other hand, had increased in value by 17.2 percent—a result that lost only some of its luster when compared with the performance of the one broker who bested her with a stock selection that gained 17.4 percent.

Also in 1982, the seasoned psi investigators Russell Targ and Keith Harary turned their attention to psychic money-making. With a third partner, California investor Anthony R. White, they formed Delphi Associates, a firm designed to convert parapsychological findings into hard cash. Their first venture, to predict the course of the silver futures market, proved profitable, they said. But later, when they tried for higher stakes, things turned sour. "It was," said White, "a difficult blow for all of us."

Delphi Associates also expressed interest in another business application of ESP—locating oil and mineral deposits. And there was a strong indication that human psychic power could do at least as well at such potentially lucrative searches as could other methods. In a survey of all the oil fields discovered in the United States from the 1880s to the 1960s,

Peter Sutcliffe (left), the Yorkshire Ripper, turned out to be a truck driver working for a company whose name began with the letter C, just as psychic Nella Jones foretold. She was also correct about his first name, though she missed the mark on several other particulars, including his appearance—as shown by her sketch of him (opposite). Skeptics contend some of Jones's so-called hits were no more than inferences that recycled old news.

CLARK Transport

T & R H CLARK (HOLDINGS) LTD.

Nella Jones (above) claimed a clairvoyant vision of the Ripper's house. Well before the killer was identified, she said he lived in a large home in Bradford, No. 6 on its street. The address was, in fact, No. 6 Garden Lane, Bradford (right). She added that the house was elevated above the street behind wrought-iron gates and had steps leading up to its front door—all true. Other would-be psychic detectives on the case misidentified the killer's hometown and tended to place him in far less savory quarters—usually in cramped slum dwellings.

A dowser hunts for water with a forked stick. On reaching its target, the stick should point sharply toward the earth.

Dowsing: The Psi Connection

Practitioners of the age-old art of dowsing seldom speculate on how the phenomenon works. They contend only that it does work—that a person can find water or any number of other subterranean or submerged items with no more than a forked stick or a bent rod as a guide. Prehistoric rock paintings in Algeria suggest that humans dowsed before they could write. Ancient Chinese and Egyptians may have used the search method as well, though written accounts of dowsing do not appear until the Middle Ages. Whatever the origins of dowsing, there is no doubt that the practice is widely done today—and with considerable apparent success.

One attempt at a physical explanation holds that dowsing works because some force emanating from un-seen objects transmits itself to the instruments used by the dowsers or to the dowsers themselves. The force has been variously and vaguely described as emissions, vibrations, electromagnetic waves, or radiation. But this theory fails to explain map dowsing, in which the dowser eschews walking over terrain with a forked stick in favor of dangling a pendulum over a map. In successful map dowsing, the pendulum swings or spins vigorously to indicate the location of whatever is being sought.

Map dowsing argues for a psychic explanation of dowsing as a whole. The psychic theory posits that the dowser's stimulation is not external but arises in some mysterious way from consciousness itself. That is, the individual's mind attunes itself to a universal pool of consciousness. Responding to information from this cosmic matrix, the dowser's muscles react involuntarily to cause a wand to dive or a pendulum to rotate. The instrument might act as an amplifier for the information or perhaps only as a focal point for the dowser's concentration. In fact, some dowsers use no instrument at all. They simply "know" where to find what they seek.

Traditionally, the principal use of dowsing has been to locate water. However, the psychic notion that all objects, animate and inanimate, project a so-called aura, or energy field, coincides with some dowsers' belief that their art can be used to find almost anything—oil, buried treasure, archeological relics, lost possessions, and even missing people.

Do-it-yourself dowsing with ordinary coat hangers

Alternative instruments to dowsing's forked stick are two metal rods, which can easily be made from a pair of wire coat hangers. Operating without official sanction, Marines sometimes employed similar devices in Vietnam to locate enemy tunnels and buried weapons. Seasoned dowsers recommend the use of the rods as follows:

Grasp the short ends lightly, holding the long ends parallel to each other and to the ground *(right)*. As you walk over the search area, hold a mental question about what you seek. If you are looking for water, for instance, keep asking: "Is there water here?" The rods will indicate a positive response by swinging away from each other to either side or swinging together and intersecting.

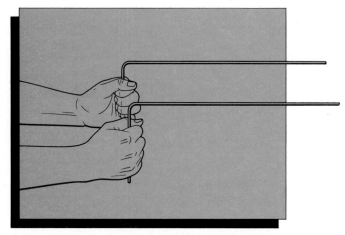

Searching: rods parallel the ground and each other.

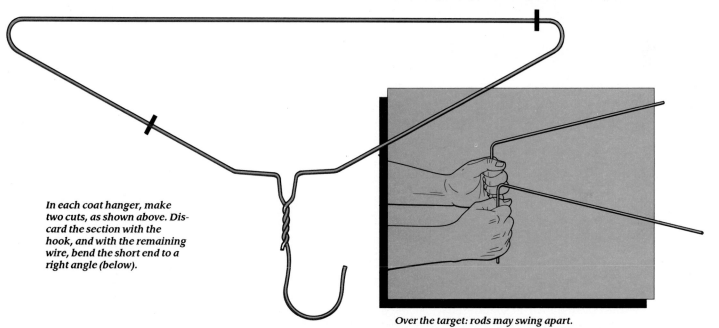

In each coat hanger, make two cuts, as shown above. Discard the section with the hook, and with the remaining wire, bend the short end to a right angle (below).

Over the target: rods may swing apart.

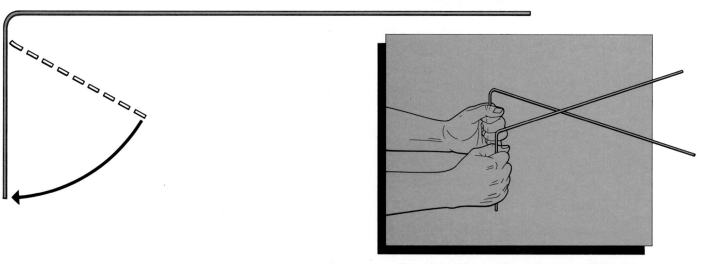

Alternate positive reaction: rods cross and intersect.

geologist H. William Menard had found that the scientific methods—test drilling and magnetometer and seismographic studies—were about as effective as "what would have been achieved had the sedimentary basins been drilled at random."

But it was the Israeli psychic-showman Uri Geller who got the most widespread credit—and, by his own account, earned the most money—for psychic explorations into oil and mineral locations. According to Geller, he pinpointed a major coal deposit for South Africa's Anglo-Transvaal mining company simply by indicating a spot on a map. Many oil companies, he reported, have used him as an "airborne divining rod," flying him over suspected oil fields until he gets a feel for where a well should be drilled. Whatever the facts of his psychic involvement with the world of commerce and industry, Geller is making a good living at it and predicts that a comfortable future lies ahead. "Big businesses," he has said, "are beginning to listen to people who think they can deliver something with their sixth senses."

Like police departments and corporations, national governments have also found the potential payoffs from extrasensory perception too attractive to ignore—despite the possibilities of failure and, even worse, embarrassment. Thus, psychic powers have been enlisted in the contest between the United States and the Soviet Union. As recently as the spring of 1987, in fact, a group of U.S. government officials reportedly assembled in an obscure room of the Capitol to hear Uri Geller tell what he knew about Soviet psychic development.

The psychic arms race first heated up in February of 1960, when the French magazine *Science et Vie* reported that the United States government had been successful in sending and receiving telepathic messages. Twice a day for sixteen days during the previous July, according to the story, a Duke University student at a laboratory near Baltimore had attempted to transmit visual impressions by telepathy to another individual. The second man, who at the appointed times concentrated on receiving the messages and drew the images he thought were being sent, was reported to be submerged at sea aboard the submarine *Nautilus*. According to the French story, the images drawn on board the submarine corresponded to the visual impressions being sent from Baltimore 70 percent of the time. The inference was that a potent new military capability—communications that were undetectable, unstoppable, and unlimited—was about to be deployed.

The United States quickly denied the story: The skipper of the *Nautilus* observed that the ship had not yet left the dock during the time of the supposed tests. Later, the author of the article said he had determined that the story was a hoax and regretted publishing it. But the denials only convinced the Soviets that something was going on. "It caused quite a turmoil," said a refugee Soviet physicist who was a graduate student at the time. "The name *Nautilus* was on everybody's lips."

No one was more delighted with the *Nautilus* tale than

the highly respected Soviet physiologist, Leonid Vasiliev. To the sixty-eight-year-old chairman of physiology at the University of Leningrad, holder of the Lenin Prize and member of the Soviet Academy of Medicine, the fact that the Americans were experimenting with ESP for military use was neither shocking nor disheartening. It was cause for celebration.

Vasiliev had been quietly researching telepathy, especially the effects of mental suggestions at a distance, since the 1920s. Marxist orthodoxy denied the existence of anything connected with a spiritual world, and the study of psychic powers was forbidden as counterrevolutionary. Now Vasiliev saw that reports of American competition, along with the promise of military benefit, could lead to a renaissance. "We must again plunge into the exploration of this vital field," he declared at a scientific conference shortly after publication of the French article. "The discovery of the energy underlying ESP will be equivalent to the discovery of atomic energy."

Vasiliev soon received official approval from the faculty of the University of Leningrad to head a special parapsychology laboratory for telepathic phenomena. Just as the launch of the Soviet satellite *Sputnik* in 1957 had energized the Ameri-

can space program, so the spurious story of the *Nautilus* experiment stimulated the Soviets to develop psychic weapons.

While the U.S. had not conducted the experiment that started the furor, neither had it been ignoring the possibilities of psychic contributions to the cold war. As early as 1952, the State Department was experimenting with exercises to increase the intuitive powers of certain employees. That same year, an internal Central Intelligence Agency memorandum recommended pushing psychic research "in the direction of reliable applications to the practical problems of intelligence."

But the official dabbling remained casual until reports of progress began to leak from the Soviet Union. Then a small-scale but classic arms race began to develop, with each side reacting to what it was afraid the other was doing. This see-saw process got its next major impetus with the publication of a book titled *Psychic Discoveries Behind the Iron Curtain*.

During the mid-1960s, freelance journalists Sheila Ostrander and Lynn Schroeder reported that they found increasing evidence of Soviet psychic research. In academic conferences and journals, some of the leading intellectuals of the country were discussing possible applications of telepathy,

Declassified documents from the Defense Intelligence Agency indicate American concern over psi research in the Eastern bloc. Nevertheless, sporadic rumors of massive U.S. spending aimed at winning the so-called psi war remain only that—rumors.

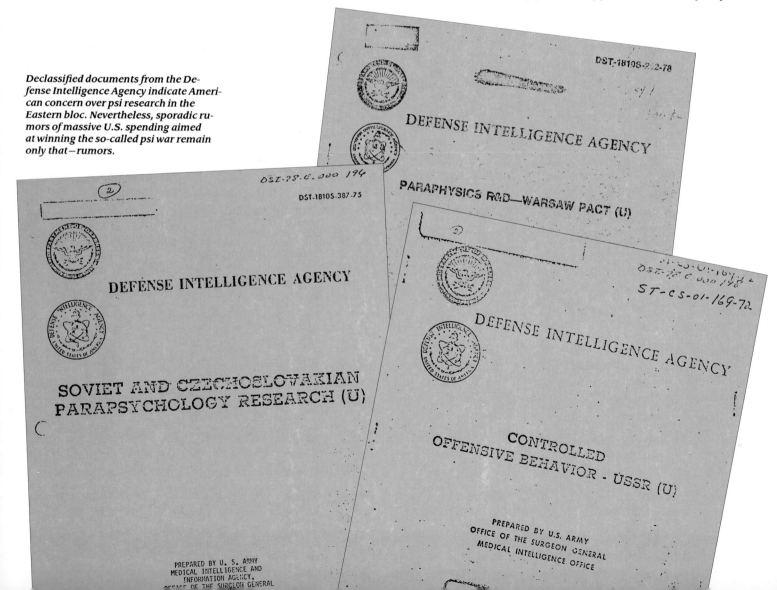

rejecting Marxist criticism of psychic research, and urging further work on parapsychology.

The two writers began to follow the subject, communicated with Soviet parapsychologists, and in 1967 attended an international ESP conference in Moscow. It was hosted by Soviet biologist Eduard Naumov, whom they later described as one of the "guiding energies of Soviet parapsychology." The writers said they eventually collected more than 300 pounds of research materials, and in 1970 they published their book.

Ostrander and Schroeder claimed the U.S. was "fifty years behind the Russians in psychic research." The Soviets were spending as much as $21 million a year on parapsychology research, while the U.S. had allocated virtually nothing. The popular book—it went to at least five hardback and thirteen paperback printings—stimulated American interest in psychic warfare.

At the same time, the book may have curtailed the Soviet program. Angered that Naumov had given so much information to foreigners, the Soviets refused to allow him to run a subsequent conference. Eventually the government decided that Naumov had revealed military secrets and sentenced him to two years in a labor camp. He was released after serving half his sentence but was not allowed to resume his work. Soviet parapsychology research ostensibly came to a halt.

Meanwhile, the book helped convince many influential Americans that the Soviets had the upper hand and that the U.S. had better catch up. Money began to flow, at least three major reports on the status of Soviet efforts were commissioned by government agencies, and publication of the results during the following few years helped heighten concern.

In the words of a 1972 study conducted by the Office of the Surgeon General, Russian success in the field might permit the Soviets to "know the contents of top secret U.S. Documents, the deployment of our troops and ships, and the location and nature of our military installations; mold the thoughts of key U.S. military and civilian leaders, at a distance; cause the instant death of any U.S. official, at a distance"; or "disable, at a distance, U.S. military equipment of all types, including spacecraft." Such darkly fanciful prospects apparently encouraged the military to go beyond the study of Soviet efforts and pursue its own research. The main beneficiary of this initiative was California's Stanford Research Institute, which in the mid-1970s received several contracts to study the applications of psychic abilities.

The U.S. Navy engaged SRI to try to determine whether psychics could detect remote sources of electromagnetic energy. If so, they could help in the difficult task of tracking deeply submerged enemy submarines. SRI claimed that the tests, which involved asking psychics to sense when a light was flashing in a distant room, were successful. But the 1978 report remains classified, and the navy will say nothing about it. Subsequent reports that the navy had as many as thirty-four psychics on a paid retainer to report the location of Soviet submarines were never confirmed.

The SRI researchers were occasionally embarrassed; experiments involving Uri Geller were later said to be characterized by "incredible sloppiness," and the institute failed to deliver on an $80,000 NASA contract to develop a machine that could teach astronauts to use ESP. But the work kept coming, and in 1973, SRI took on its most celebrated assignment—Project Scanate. The mission: to study remote-viewing techniques for the Central Intelligence Agency.

Russell Targ and Harold Puthoff, the two physicists who had become leading researchers at SRI, conducted the experiments. Working primarily with the well-known psychic Ingo Swann and retired police official Pat Price, they staged a number of tests of the psychics' ability to view distant locales.

During one session, which was closely monitored by the CIA, Price gave a detailed description of a secret, underground military facility in Virginia. Asked to project himself there again and look for information about code words, Price recited nine words or phrases that he said were on papers on top of a desk and on file folders inside a cabinet. He also gave the names and ranks of three of the installation's top officers.

The government, of course, did not publicly confirm Price's disclosures. But according to a later report, security officials at the installation—the function of which was to eavesdrop on Soviet satellites—conducted an investigation to

find out how Price had got the information. He, meanwhile, had obligingly gone on to describe a similar Soviet listening post in the Ural Mountains half a world away.

Some critics insisted that Project Scanate was a totally worthless enterprise, and support for such efforts began to wane. Samuel Koslov, the navy's assistant secretary for research and development, pronounced SRI's psychic investigations a waste of taxpayers' money and ordered the navy's contracts with the firm cancelled. But new life was soon injected into the so-called psi war controversy by the Soviets—in an incident that was either a clumsy blunder on their part or a clever bit of manipulation. It began in June of 1977 with a phone call from Soviet biophysicist Valery Petukhov to Robert Toth, Moscow correspondent for the *Los Angeles Times*. Petukhov offered Toth a news release containing the latest information about Soviet research into parapsychology, and Toth agreed to meet him on a Moscow street. But when Toth accepted a twenty-page document, both men were rushed by KGB officers, arrested, and taken away for questioning.

Accused of receiving state secrets about parapsychology, Toth was interrogated at length but eventually released. In trying to explain to his newspaper what the flap had been about, the reporter said he had learned that "the Russians were trying to use extrasensory perception and other psychic phenomena for military purposes." Toth had not been particularly interested in parapsychology: "It seemed laughable until now," he said. But the Soviets, by accident or design, had reminded many Americans of the subject—and convinced many of their presumed lead in psychic-weapons research.

The U.S. Defense Department continued to deny, as it always had and still does, any interest in psychic matters. But the denials appear to be exercises in semantics: One 1978 study, titled "Novel Biological Information Transfer Systems," was in fact a report on Soviet ESP. At any rate, occasional revelations continued to testify to continued military and intelligence-community concern about psychic weapons.

Confirmation came in the December 1980 issue of *Military Review*, the professional journal of the United States Army. The issue contained articles on such things as the strategic implications of deploying the Pershing II missile in Europe and the administrative logistics of war readiness. Included, too, was a dissertation with an intriguing, two-level title—"The New Mental Battlefield: Beam Me Up, Spock"—that suggested military scholarship while referring to a popular science-fiction television series.

The writer, Lieutenant Colonel John B. Alexander, stated flatly that "there are weapons systems that operate on the power of the mind and whose lethal capacity has already been demonstrated." He discussed the ability to transmit disease over distance and said that illness or death had been successfully induced in lower organisms such as flies and frogs. "The present capacity for human death," he said, "is still debated."

Nationally syndicated columnist Jack Anderson responded to the colonel's article with a pair of columns reporting that the U.S. was using psychics "to spy on the Soviets by projecting their minds outside their bodies" and that the CIA was considering deploying "psychic shields" to protect American secrets from the Soviets. The columns, researched by Anderson's associate Ron McRae, ridiculed such "futuristic fantasies" and "voodoo warfare." In the wake of the frenzy produced by the columns, the Soviet Embassy put out a rare press release trumpeting its achievements in psychic warfare; and McRae went to work writing a book on the subject.

There is little in the record of psychic contributions to the military—as is the case with academia, criminal justice, and finance—to convert a believer or a nonbeliever. Skeptics cannot totally discredit every favorable psychic result, and the most ardent enthusiast cannot claim consistent success. But the successes are reported often enough, and the potential rewards are great enough, to encourage repeated attempts.

In the midst of the flap over Anderson's columns, while busily denying any Defense Department involvement with psychic warfare, Pentagon publicists posted a reminder about the danger of unqualified pronouncements on such subjects. It was a statement made by Admiral William Leahy, chief of staff to President Roosevelt during World War II. "The A-bomb is the biggest fool thing," said Leahy in early 1945. "The bomb will never go off and I speak as an expert on explosives."

The Kirlian Effect

In 1939, a Soviet electrician named Semyon Kirlian was working at a hospital in the city of Krasnodar when he happened to see a high-frequency physiotherapy machine in operation. A spark jumped between an electrode and the patient's skin, and Kirlian, a part-time inventor, wondered how the spark might appear if photographed. To find out, he fixed electrodes to one of his hands, pressed it onto a photographic plate, and pulled a switch. He burned his hand. But when he processed the film, he found his handprint surrounded by a halo similar to the one shown above. From this serendipitous event sprang a new use of the photographic medium—one that would hold great interest for parapsychologists.

Several methods are used in Kirlian photography, as the process is called. A typical one involves putting film atop a flat metal plate. An object is placed on the film and photographed while a high-voltage electrical charge pulses through the plate. No camera is involved. Animate subjects produce auras that vary in color, size, and shape in sequential photographs; inanimate objects display more regular, unvarying halos. Some examples appear on the following pages.

Kirlian photography enjoyed a vogue in the United States during the 1970s. Some enthusiasts contended it confirmed at last the aura psychics had long described surrounding living things. They also believed that these auras, or so-called Kirlian effects, revealed clues to an individual's emotions and physiology. Skeptics argued that the auras were only a sort of "laboratory lightning" created by electrically ionized air.

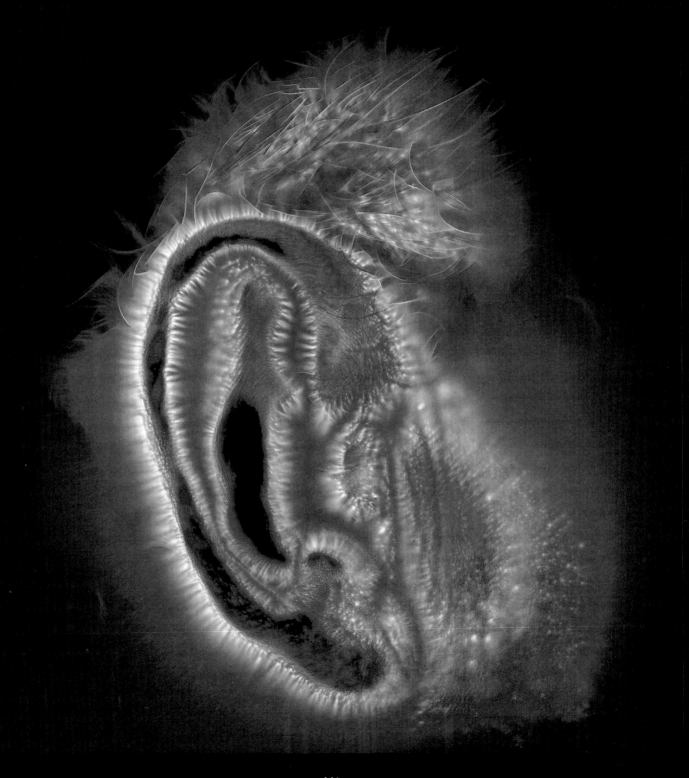

Red, white, and blue, typical in Kirlian color photos, predominate in this picture of a human ear. Kirlian enthusiasts call the halos auras; scientists prefer "corona discharge imagings."

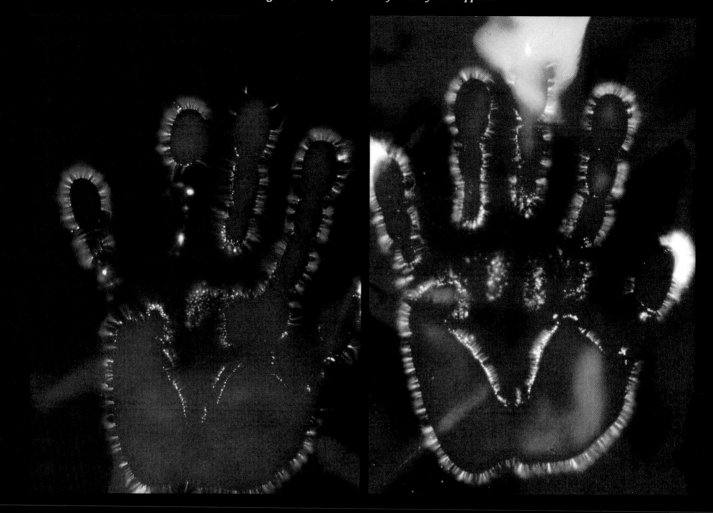

The hand of psychic Olga Worrall is shown in its normal state (left) and while trying to generate healing energy. In this heightened state, red intensifies and yellow appears.

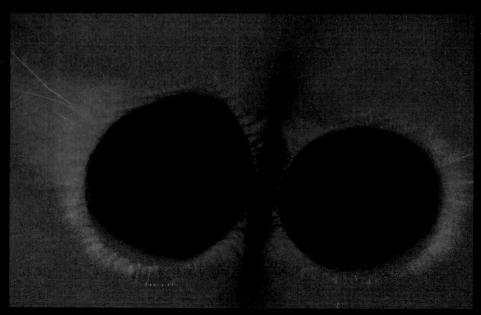

Two individuals' fingertips appear as black dots with auras from blue to red. The black between the corona patterns is said to reflect an emotional barrier between the two persons.

Daisy petals shoot white rays through a violet glow.

Psi proponents say the rare "phantom leaf" phenomenon hints at a mysterious energy matrix holding templates for all life. The tip of the ivy leaf shown below was severed before it was photographed, yet the missing part persists in the picture as an afterimage. Critics say the whole leaf is pressed onto the film before any part is amputated, and the "ghost" is residue from the severed section. Most serious investigators insist the leaf is cut before any part of it touches the film.

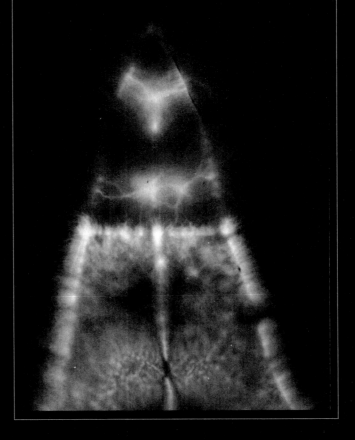

A majestic white and blue-violet aura surrounds an elderberry leaf.

*A drop of tangerine juice appears as a mottled black
and red circle with a pink and white aura and radiating white tendrils. Supposedly, each
different fruit juice has a unique Kirlian pattern.*

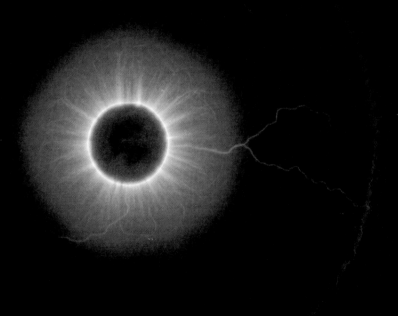

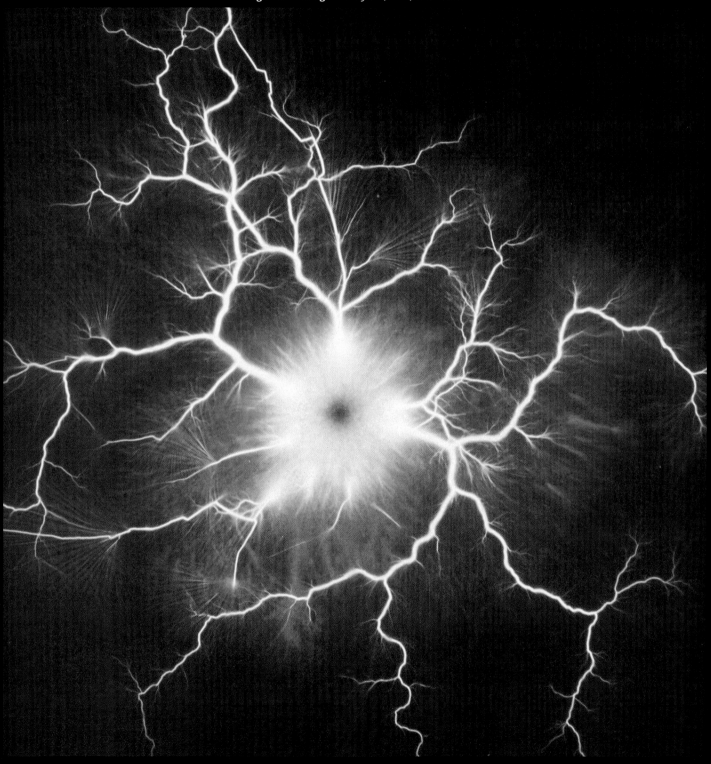

*In this Kirlian photograph, a steel ball dropped on a
high-energy field becomes a deep pink circle, projecting spectacular lightninglike rays
against a background of red, blue, and violet.*

ACKNOWLEDGMENTS

The index was prepared by Lynne R. Hobbs. The translations of the quotations of Stefan Ossowiecki and Stanislaw Poniatowksi that appear on pages 121-122 of this volume are taken from *The Secret Vaults of Time,* © 1978 by Stephan A. Schwartz, and are reprinted with the author's permission.

The editors wish to thank: Dorothy Allison, Nutley, N.J.; American Society of Dowsers, Danville, Vt.; Jean-Claude Arrati, St. Cloud, France; Professor Hans Bender, Director, Institut für Grenzgebiete der Psychologie und Psychohygiene, Freiburg, West Germany; Richard Bennett, Winnipeg, Canada; Christopher Bird, Molokai, Hawaii; Richard S. Broughton, Foundation for Research on the Nature of Man, Durham, N.C.; Adam Chism, Springfield, Va.; Jerome Clarke, *Fate,* Highland Park, Ill.; Marie-Véronique Clin, Directeur Adjoint, Centre Jeanne D'Arc, Orléans, France; Eileen Coley, Director, Parapsychology Foundation, New York; Brenda J. Dunne, Princeton, N.J.; Patric V. Giesler, Dept. of Anthropology, Brandeis University, Waltham, Mass.; Paola Giovetti, Modena, Italy; Keith Harary, Institute for Advanced Pyschology, San Francisco; Charles Honorton, Psychophysical Research Lab, Princeton, N.J.; Irene Hughes, Chicago; Peter Hurkos, Studio City, Calif.; Joicey Hurth, Cedarburg, Wis.; Robert G. Jahn, Princeton University, Princeton, N.J.; William Kautz, Center for Applied Intuition, San Francisco; Stanley Krippner, Saybrook Institute, San Francisco; Emilio Lorenzo, Gif-Sur-Yvette, France; Robert Lund, American Museum of Magic, Marshall, Mich.; Donna McCormick, American Society for Psychical Research, New York; Mankind Research Foundation, Silver Spring, Md.; Lewis Matacia, Dunn Loring, Va.; Jørgen Meldgaard, National Museum, Copenhagen; Thelma Moss, North Hollywood, Calif.; R. Jeff Munson, Foundation on the Nature of Man, Durham, N.C.; National Spiritual Science Center, Washington, D.C.; H. E. Puthoff, Institute for Advanced Studies, Austin, Tex.; James Randi, Sunrise, Fla.; Milan Ryzl, San Jose, Calif.; Jean-Claude Secondé, Président du Centre Français du Magnétisme, Paris; Giorgio di Simone, Centro Italiano di Parapsicologia, Naples; Rolf Streichardt, Institut für Grenzgebiete der Psychologie und Psychohygiene, Freiburg, West Germany; Russell Targ, Lockheed Research and Development, Palo Alto, Calif.; Jeanette Thomas, Edgar Cayce Foundation, Virginia Beach, Va.; Jean Tixier, Ingénier E.C.P., Sainte Catherine de Fierbois, France; Susana Valadez, Huichol Center for Cultural Survival and Traditonal Arts, Oakland, Calif.; Jean-Marie Vergério, Grand Conseiller de L'Ordre de la Rose-Croix, A.M.O.R.C., Paris; Maria de Via-Lorenzo, Gif-Sur-Yvette, France; Alberto Villoldo, Four Winds Foundation, Sausalito, Calif.; Timothy White, editor, *Shaman's Drum,* Berkeley, Calif.; and in England: David Bronwich, Robert Cracknell, Hilary Evans, Melvin Harris, John Lindsay, Jo Logan, Steve Speed, Roy Stemmon, and John Christopher Travers.

PICTURE CREDITS

The sources for the pictures in this book are listed below. Credits for pictures shown from left to right are separated by semicolons; credits from top to bottom are separated by dashes.

Cover: Art by Jack Pardue. 7: Art by Wendy Popp, detail of picture on pages 12, 13. 8-13: Art by Wendy Popp. 15: Art by Alfred T. Kamajian. 16: Mark Twain Home Board, Hannibal, Mo. 18: Roger-Viollet, Paris. 19: Art by Linda Benson. 22, 23: Art by Jeffrey Adams. 24, 25: From *Mental Radio* by Upton Sinclair, Charles C Thomas, 1962, Springfield, Ill., except bottom right, © David Sinclair, courtesy Lilly Library, Indiana University, Bloomington, Ind. 26: Mary Evans Picture Library, London/© Sigmund Freud; © Philippe Halsman. 27: Ron Galella. 28, 29: Courtesy Society for Psychical Research, London. 30, 31: Sygma; Woods Hole Oceanographic Institute. 32, 33: John Topham Picture Library, Edenbridge, Kent. 35: Courtesy American Society for Psychical Research, detail of photo on page 44. 36-39: Courtesy American Society for Psychical Research. 40: Department of Archives and Special Collections, University of Manitoba, courtesy American Society for Psychical Research; courtesy American Society for Psychical Research. 41: Department of Archives and Special Collections, University of Manitoba, courtesy American Society for Psychical Research. 42-47: Courtesy American Society for Psychical Research. 49: Art by Alfred T. Kamajian. 51, 52: Courtesy Foundation for Research on the Nature of Man. 54, 55: NASA; courtesy Foundation for Research on the Nature of Man; NASA. 57: © Estate of C. G. Jung, courtesy Manuscript Department, William R. Perkins Library, Duke University. 58, 59: Fred Bruemmer; Merlin D. Tuttle, Bat Conservation International — David Doubilet. 60: Kenneth Lee. 61: Hella Hammid. 62: Courtesy Russell Targ (2) — Howard Sochurek — courtesy Keith Harary, Ph.D. (2). 63: Courtesy Grant L. Robertson (3) — courtesy Russell Targ (2). 64, 65: Milan Ryzl; art by Bobbi Tull. 66: National Institute of Mental Health. 67: Henry Groskinsky. 68, 69: Henry Groskinsky, courtesy Psychophysical Research Lab — Cameron Davidson/Bruce Coleman; Michal Heron. 70-73: Art by Douglas R. Chezem. 75: Jack Savage, courtesy Western Historical Manuscript Collection, detail of drawing on page 79. 76, 77: National Museum of Denmark, Department of Ethnology. 78: Jack Savage, courtesy Western Historical Manuscript Collection (2)—Joint Collection, University of Missouri, Western Historical Manuscript Collection, Columbia State Historical Society of Missouri Manuscripts. 79: Jack Savage, courtesy Western Historical Manuscript Collection. 80: Susana Eger Valadez. 81: Mariano Valadez, © 1986 *Shaman's Drum.* 83: Art by Alfred T. Kamajian. 85: Henry Groskinsky. 86: Courtesy Ingo Swann. 88, 89: Mary Evans Picture Library, London/Society for Psychical Research. 90, 91: Edgar Cayce Foundation. 92-101: Kay Ritchie, London. 103: Theater Arts Library, Harry Ransom Humanities Research Center, University of Texas at Austin. 104: From *Confidences d'un Prestidigitateur* by Jean Eugène Robert-Houdin, Lecesne, 1858, Blois, courtesy Bibliothèque Nationale, Paris. 105: Courtesy General Research Division, The New York Public Library, Astor, Lenox and Tilden Foundation. 106: Dick Stevens, courtesy Robert Lund, American Museum of Magic; courtesy C. McCord Purdy. 107, 108: Dick Stevens, courtesy Robert Lund, American Museum of Magic. 109: Mary Evans Picture Library, London/Harry Price Collection, University of London. 110: UPI/Bettmann; Milbourne Christopher Collection—Harry Price Collection, University of London. 111: Harry Price Collection, University of London.

BIBLIOGRAPHY

Abell, George O., and Barry Singer, eds., *Science and the Paranormal.* New York: Charles Scribner's Sons, 1983.

Adamenko, Victor G., "Memories of Semyon Kirlian." *International Journal of Paraphysics* (Paris), Volume 13, Issues 1 and 2, 1979.

Agee, Doris, *Edgar Cayce on ESP.* New York: Castle Books, 1969.

Allison, Dorothy, and Scott Jacobson, *Dorothy Allison: A Psychic Story.* New York: Jove, 1980.

American Society for Psychical Research, *Proceedings of the American Society for Psychical Research: The Margery Mediumship.* Vol. 2. New York: ASPR, 1933.

Barker, J. C., "Premonitions of the Aberfan Disaster." *Journal of the Society for Psychical Research,* December 1967.

Barrett, W. P., ed. and transl., *The Trial of Jeanne D'Arc.* New York: Gotham House, 1932.

Barrett, Sir William, and Theodore Besterman, *The Divining Rod.* Toronto: Coles, 1979.

Bartlett, Laile E., *Psi Trek.* New York: McGraw-Hill, 1981.

Berrin, Kathleen, ed., *Art of the Huichol Indians.* New York: Harry N. Abrams, 1978.

Bird, Christopher, *The Divining Hand.* New York: E. P. Dutton, 1979.

Blackburn, Douglas:
"Confessions of a Famous Medium." *John Bull* (London), December 5, 1908.
"Confessions of a Telepathist." *Daily News* (London), September 1, 1911.

Blodgett, Jean, *The Coming and Going of the Shaman.* Show catalogue. Winnipeg: Winnipeg Art Gallery, March 11-June 11, 1978.

Bond, Frederick Bligh, *The Gate of Remembrance.* New York: E. P. Dutton, 1933.

"Boom Times on the Psychic Frontier." *Time,* March 4, 1974.

Booth, John, *Psychic Paradoxes.* Buffalo: Prometheus Books, 1986.

Bradbury, Will, ed., *Into the Unknown.* Pleasantville, N.Y.: Reader's Digest Association, 1981.

Branston, Brian, *Beyond Belief.* New York: Walker, 1974.

Brian, Denis, *The Enchanted Voyager: The Life of J. B. Rhine.* Englewood Cliffs, N.J.: Prentice-Hall, 1982.

Browning, Norma Lee, *The Psychic World of Peter Hurkos.* Garden City, N.Y.: Doubleday, 1970.

Burrows, Robert J. L., "Americans Get Religion in the New Age." *Christianity Today,* May 16, 1986.

"The Case of ESP." *(NOVA* television series transcript, Program 1101). Boston: WGBH Educational Foundation, January 17, 1984.

Cavendish, Richard, ed., *Man, Myth & Magic.* Vol. 3. New York: Marshall Cavendish, 1985.

Christopher, Milbourne:
ESP, Seers & Psychics. New York: Thomas Y. Crowell, 1970.
The Illustrated History of Magic. New York: Thomas Y. Crowell, 1973.

Colligan, Douglas, "The Kirlian Connection: The Future of Electro-Photography in Medicine and Technology." *Science Digest,* November 1976.

Cox, Robert V., and Kenneth L. Peiffer, Jr., *Missing Person.* Harrisburg, Pa.: Stackpole Books, 1979.

Dean, Douglas, et al., *Executive ESP.* Englewood Cliffs, N.J.: Prentice-Hall, 1974.

Douglas, Alfred, *Extra-Sensory Powers.* Woodstock, N.Y.: Overlook Press, 1977.

Drury, Nevill, *The Shaman and the Magician.* London: Routledge & Kegan Paul, 1982.

Ebon, Martin:
Psychic Warfare: Threat or Illusion? New York: McGraw-Hill, 1983.
They Knew the Unknown. New York: World, 1971.

Edelson, Edward, "Ghost Images of Kirlian Photography Puzzle Experts." *Smithsonian,* April 1977.

Edge, Hoyt L., et al., *Foundations of Parapsychology.* Boston: Routledge & Kegan Paul, 1986.

Eliade, Mircea, *Shamanism: Archaic Techniques of Ecstasy.* Transl. by Willard R. Trask. Princeton, N.J.: Princeton University Press, 1974.

Fairley, John, and Simon Welfare, *Arthur C. Clarke's World of Strange Powers.* New York: G. P. Putnam's Sons, 1984.

Fisher, Allan C., Jr., "Mysteries of Bird Migration." *National Geographic,* August 1979.

Frank, Gerold, *The Boston Strangler.* New York: New American Library, 1966.

Frazier, Kendrick, "The Case of Remote Viewing: Transcripts, Finally Released, Are Filled with Cues." *Skeptical Inquirer* (Buffalo), summer 1986.

Friedman, Joe, "Freud's Guilty Secret." *The Unexplained* (London), Volume 13, Issue 148.

Gardner, Martin:
"Einstein and ESP." *The Zetetic* (Buffalo), fall-winter 1977.
"Notes of a Psi-Watcher." *Skeptical Inquirer* (Buffalo), fall 1983.

Garrett, Eileen J.:
Many Voices. New York: G. P. Putnam's Sons, 1968.
Telepathy: In Search of a Lost Faculty. New York: Helix Press, 1974.

Geller, Uri, and Guy Lyon Playfair, *The Geller Effect.* London: Jonathan Cape, 1986.

Goodman, Jeffrey, *Psychic Archaeology.* New York: Berkeley, 1977.

Grattan-Guinness, Ivor, ed., *Psychical Research.* Wellingborough, Northamptonshire, England: Aquarian Press, 1982.

Graves, Tom, *The Diviner's Handbook.* New York: Destiny Books, 1986.

Greeley, Andrew, "Mysticism Goes Mainstream." *American Health,* January-February 1987.

Greenhouse, Herbert B., *Premonitions: A Leap into the Future.* New York: Bernard Geis Associates, 1971.

Gris, Henry, and William Dick, *The New Soviet Psychic Discoveries.* Englewood Cliffs, N.J.: Prentice-Hall, 1978.

Halifax, Joan:
Shaman: The Wounded Healer. New York: Crossroad, 1982.
Shamanic Voices. New York: E. P. Dutton, 1979.

Hamilton, David K., Rhea A. White, and Linda Henkel, "Centennial Compilation of the Contents of the *Proceedings* and *Journal of the American Society for Psychical Research* 1885-1984: Part 1: 1885-1910." *Journal of the American Society for Psychical Research* (New York), January 1985.

Hansel, C. E. M., *ESP and Parapsychology: A Critical Reevaluation.* Buffalo: Prometheus Books, 1980.

Hardy, Alister, Robert Harvie, and Arthur Koestler, *The Challenge of Chance.* New York: Random House, 1973.

Hibbard, Whitney S., and Raymond W. Worring, *Psychic Criminology.* Springfield, Ill.: Charles C Thomas, 1982.

Hitching, Francis, *Dowsing: The Psi Connection.* Garden City, N.Y.: Anchor Books, 1978.

Holroyd, Stuart:
Dream Worlds. Garden City, N.Y.: Doubleday, 1976.
Minds without Boundaries. Garden City, N.Y.: Doubleday, 1976.
Psychic Voyages. Garden City, N.Y.: Doubleday, 1977.

Holzer, Hans, *The Truth about ESP.* Garden City, N.Y.: Doubleday, 1974.

Hopkins, Joseph M., "Experts on Nontraditional Religions Try to Pin Down the New Age Movement." *Christianity Today,* May 16, 1986.

Hurkos, Peter, *Psychic.* Indianapolis: Bobbs-Merrill Company, 1961.

Ireland, William Henry, ed., *Memoirs of Jeanne D'Arc.* London: Robert Triphook, 1824.

Jahn, Robert G., "The Persistent Paradox of Psychic Phenomena: An Engineering Perspective." *Proceedings of the Institute of Electrical and Electronics Engineers,* February 1982.

Jay, Ricky, *Learned Pigs & Fireproof Women.* New York: Villard Books, 1986.

Johnson, Kendall, *The Living Aura.* New York: Hawthorn Books, 1975.

Jones, Carol, "Photos Show How Faith Can Heal." *Prevention,* December 1973.

Jones, David E., *Visions of Time.* Wheaton, Ill.: Theosophical, 1979.

Jung, Carl G., *Man and His Symbols.* Garden City, N.Y.: Doubleday, 1983.

Kanigel, Robert, "Why Dream?" *Science 85,* December 1985.

Kenawell, William W., *The Quest at Glastonbury.* New York: Helix Press, 1965.

"Kirlian Electrophotography." Washington: Mankind Research Unlimited, 1974.

Krippner, Stanley, *Human Possibilities.* Garden City, N.Y.: Anchor Press/Doubleday, 1980.

Krippner, Stanley, and Daniel Rubin, eds., *The Energies of Consciousness: Explorations in Acupuncture, Auras, and Kirlian Photography.* New York: Gordon and Breach, 1975.

Kurtz, Paul, ed., *A Skeptic's Handbook of Parapsychology.* Buffalo: Prometheus Books, 1985.

Levine, Art, Cynthia Kyle, and Peter Dworkin, "Mystics on Main Street." *U.S. News & World Report,* February 9, 1987.

Long, Joseph K., ed., *Extrasensory Ecology: Parapsychology and Anthropology.* Metuchen, N.J.: Scarecrow Press, 1977.

McKean, Kevin, "In Search of the Unconscious Mind." *Discover,* February 1985.

MacKenzie, Andrew, *The Unexplained.* London: Arthur Barker, 1966.

MacLean, Gordon, *A Field Guide to Dowsing.* Danville, Vt.: American Society of Dowsers, 1976.

McRae, Ronald M., *Mind Wars: The True Story of Government Research into the Military Potential of Psychic Weapons.* New York: St. Martin's Press, 1984.

Macrory, Patrick, "A Time Traveller." *Society for Psychical Research Newsletter Supplement* (London), October 1986.

Marks, David, and Richard Kammann, *The Psychology of the Psychic.* Buffalo: Prometheus Books, 1980.

Mauskopf, Seymour H., and Michael R. McVaugh, *The Elusive Science.* Baltimore: Johns Hopkins University Press, 1980.

Mitchell, Edgar D., *Psychic Exploration.* New York: G. P. Putnam's Sons, 1974.

Moss, Thelma, and Ken Johnson, "Radiation Field Photography." *Psychic,* July 1972.

Murchison, Carl, ed., *The Case for and against Psychical Belief.* Worcester, Mass.: Clark University, 1927.

Nagorka, Henry J., "Bogna Sees with Her Fingers." *Psychic Observer & Chimes* (Washington), April-May-June 1975.

Neher, Andrew, *The Psychology of Transcendence.* Englewood Cliffs, N.J.: Prentice-Hall, 1980.

Neihardt, John G., *Black Elk Speaks.* New York: Pocket Books, 1972.

Oakley, E. M., "Psychic First Lady." *Psychic,* September-October 1976.

Ostrander, Sheila, and Lynn Schroeder:
Handbook of Psi Discoveries. New York: Berkeley, 1974.
Psychic Discoveries behind the Iron Curtain. Englewood Cliffs, N.J.: Prentice-Hall, 1970.

Parapsychology Review (New York). Special issue, October 1970.

Pollack, Jack Harrison, *Croiset the Clairvoyant.* Garden City, N.Y.: Doubleday, 1964.

Prince, Walter Franklin:
The Case of Patience Worth. New Hyde Park, N.Y.: University Books, 1964.
"Experiments by the Scientific American." *Journal of the American Society for Psychical Research* (New York), June 1924.
Noted Witnesses for Psychic Occurrences. New Hyde Park, N.Y.: University Books, 1963.

Randi, James:
Flim-Flam! Buffalo: Prometheus Books, 1982.
The Magic of Uri Geller. New York: Ballantine Books, 1975.

Rao, K. Ramakrishna, ed., *J. B. Rhine: On the Frontiers of Science.* Jefferson, N.C.: McFarland, 1982.

Rasmussen, Knud, *Intellectual Culture of the Iglulik Eskimos.* Copenhagen, Gyldendalske Boghandel, Nordisk Forlag, 1929.

Rensberger, Boyce, "False Tests Peril Psychic Research." *New York Times,* August 20, 1974.

Rhine, Louisa E., *ESP in Life and Lab.* New York: Collier Macmillan, 1967.

"The R101 Rises Again." *Alpha,* January-February 1986.

Roney-Dougal, Serena, "Telepathy: Seeing the Light." *The Unexplained* (London), Volume 9, Issue 102.

Rosenfeld, Seth, "Major Psychic 'Remote Viewing' Experiment Called Success." *San Francisco Examiner,* November 23, 1984.

Ryzl, Milan, *Hypnosis & ESP.* Chene-Bourg, Switzerland: Ariston Verlag, 1976.

Schwartz, Stephan A.:
The Alexandria Project. New York: Dell, 1983.
The Secret Vaults of Time. New York: Grosset & Dunlap, 1978.

Severn, Bill, *Magic in Mind.* New York: Henry Z. Walck, 1974.

Sherrill, Peter, "Edgar Cayce: The Man Who Saw Through Time and Space." Virginia Beach, Va.: Edgar Cayce Foundation, 1971.

Sigstedt, Cyriel Odhner, *The Swedenborg Epic.* New York: Bookman Associates, 1952.

Sinclair, Upton, *Mental Radio.* Springfield, Ill.: Charles C Thomas, 1962.

Smith, Susy, *ESP for the Millions.* Los Angeles: Sherbourne Press, 1965.

Stearn, Jess, *The Miracle Workers.* Garden City, N.Y.: Doubleday, 1972.

Steiger, Brad, *Irene Hughes on Psychic Safari.* New York: Warner, 1972.

Stemman, Roy:
"Clues from Clairvoyance." *The Unexplained* (London), Volume 1, Issue 4.
"Obeying the Inner Voice." *The Unexplained* (London), Volume 2, Issue 14.
"The Warning Voice." *The Unexplained* (London), Volume 1, Issue 6.

Stevenson, Ian, *Telepathic Impressions.* Charlottesville: University Press of Virginia, 1970.

Stone, W. Clement, and Norma Lee Browning, *The Other Side of the Mind.* Englewood Cliffs, N.J.: Prentice-Hall, 1964.

Sugrue, Thomas, *There Is a River.* New York: Henry Holt, 1956.

Swann, Ingo, *To Kiss Earth Good-Bye.* New York: Hawthorn Books, 1975.

Talbot, Michael, *Beyond the Quantum.* New York: Macmillan, 1986.

Tanous, Alex, and Harvey Ardman, *Beyond Coincidence.* Garden City, N.Y.: Doubleday, 1976.

Targ, Russell, and Keith Harary, *The Mind Race.* New York: Villard Books, 1984.

Taylor, John, *Science and the Supernatural.* New York: E. P. Dutton, 1980.

Third Report on Thought-Transference. Proceedings of the Society for Psychical Research, London, April 24, 1883.

Thompson, Gordon T., "Federal Grant Supports ESP Dream Research at Maimonides." *New York Times,* November 25, 1973.

Tietze, Thomas R., *Margery.* New York: Harper & Row, 1973.

Tinbergen, Niko, and the Editors of Life, *Animal Behavior* (Life Nature Library series). New York: Time-Life Books, 1965.

Trobridge, George, *Emanuel Swedenborg: His Life, Teachings and Influence.* New York: New-Church Press, 1919.

Tuttle, Merlin D., "The Amazing Frog-Eating Bat." *National Geographic,* January 1982.

Twain, Mark:
Life on the Mississippi. New York: Penguin Books, 1984.
Mark Twain's Autobiography. Vol. 1. New York: Harper & Brothers, 1924.

Ullman, Montague, Stanley Krippner, and Alan Vaughan, *Dream Telepathy.* New York: Macmillan, 1973.

Valadez, Susana:
"Dreams and Visions from the Gods." *Shaman's Drum* (Oakland, Calif.), fall 1986.
"Mirrors of the Gods." *Shaman's Drum* (Oakland, Calif.), fall 1986.

Warner, Marina, *Joan of Arc.* New York: Vintage Books, 1982.

Watkins, Arleen J., and William S. Bickel, "A Study of the Kirlian Effect." *Skeptical Inquirer* (Buffalo), spring 1986.

Weaver, Herbert, *Divining the Primary Sense.* London: Routledge & Kegan Paul, 1978.

White, John, and Stanley Krippner, eds., *Future Science.* Garden City, N.Y.: Anchor Books, 1977.

Wickware, Francis Sill, "Dr. Rhine & Extra-Sensory Perception." *Life,* April 15, 1940.

Wilson, Colin, *The Psychic Detectives.* San Francisco: Mercury House, 1985.

Wolman, Benjamin B., ed., *Handbook of Parapsychology.* New York: Van Nostrand Reinhold, 1977.

INDEX

Numerals in italics indicate an illustration of the subject mentioned.

Time-Life Books Inc.
is a wholly owned subsidiary of
TIME INCORPORATED

FOUNDER: Henry R. Luce 1898-1967

Editor-in-Chief: Henry Anatole Grunwald
Chairman and Chief Executive Officer: J. Richard Munro
President and Chief Operating Officer: N. J. Nicholas, Jr.
Chairman of the Executive Committee: Ralph P. Davidson
Corporate Editor: Ray Cave
Executive Vice President, Books: Kelso F. Sutton
Vice President, Books: George Artandi

TIME-LIFE BOOKS INC.

EDITOR: George Constable
Executive Editor: Ellen Phillips
Director of Design: Louis Klein
Director of Editorial Resources: Phyllis K. Wise
Editorial Board: Russell B. Adams, Jr., Dale M. Brown,
Roberta Conlan, Thomas H. Flaherty,
Lee Hassig, Donia Ann Steele, Rosalind Stubenberg,
Kit van Tulleken, Henry Woodhead
Director of Photography and Research: John Conrad Weiser

PRESIDENT: Christopher T. Linen
Chief Operating Officer: John M. Fahey, Jr.
Senior Vice Presidents: James L. Mercer, Leopoldo Toralballa
Vice Presidents: Stephen L. Bair, Ralph J. Cuomo, Neal Goff,
Stephen L. Goldstein, Juanita T. James, Hallett Johnson III,
Carol Kaplan, Susan J. Maruyama, Robert H. Smith,
Paul R. Stewart, Joseph J. Ward
Director of Production Services: Robert J. Passantino

Editorial Operations
Copy Chief: Diane Ullius
Editorial Operations Manager: Caroline A. Boubin
Production: Celia Beattie
Quality Control: James J. Cox (director)
Library: Louise D. Forstall

MYSTERIES OF THE UNKNOWN

SERIES DIRECTOR: Russell B. Adams, Jr.
Series Administrator: Elise Ritter Gibson
Designer: Herbert H. Quarmby

Editorial Staff for *Psychic Powers*
Associate Editors: Neil Kagan (pictures); Pat Daniels,
Anne Horan (text)
Writers: Janet P. Cave, Laura Foreman
Assistant Designer: Lorraine D. Rivard
Copy Coordinators: Darcie Conner Johnston,
Carolee Belkin Walker
Picture Coordinator: Bradley Hower
Editorial Assistant: Donna Fountain

Special Contributors: Christine Hinze (London, picture
research); Thomas A. Lewis, Valerie Moolman, Daniel
Stashower, Marta Vogel, Robert H. White (text); Kaila
Smith (administration)

Correspondents: Elisabeth Kraemer-Singh (Bonn); Maria
Vincenza Aloisi (Paris); Ann Natanson (Rome).
Valuable assistance was also provided by Pavle Svabic
(Belgrade), Barbara Gevene Hertz (Copenhagen), Judy
Aspinall (London), Christina Lieberman (New York), Ann
Wise (Rome), Dick Berry (Tokyo).

The research for *Psychic Powers* was prepared under the
supervision of Time-Life Books by:
Bibliographics Inc.
President: David L. Harrison
Researchers: Jill M. Denney, Isabel H. Fucigna, Martha L.
Johnson, Sydney Johnson, Sara Mark, Linda Look,
Jacqueline Shaffer, Susan Stuck, Deborah A. Thornton,
Bruce Wells
Editorial Assistant: Lona E. Tavernise

The Consultants:

Marcello Truzzi, professor of sociology at Eastern
Michigan University, is also director of the Center for
Scientific Anomalies Research (CSAR) and editor of its
journal, the *Zetetic Scholar.* Dr. Truzzi, who considers
himself a "constructive skeptic" with regard to claims of
the paranormal, works through the CSAR to produce
dialogues between critics and proponents of unusual
scientific claims.

James G. Matlock is librarian and archivist of the
American Society for Psychical Research (ASPR). He is a
member of the Parapsychological Association and has
written extensively on the history of parapsychology.

Stephan A. Schwartz is chairman and research director of
the Mobius Society, a parapsychological research
foundation located in Los Angeles. He is also author of
The Secret Vaults of Time and *The Alexandria Project,* two
books dealing with psychic archeology.

Library of Congress Cataloguing in Publication Data
Psychic powers.
(Mysteries of the unknown)
Bibliography: p.
Includes index.
1. Psychical research. I. Time-Life Books.
II. Series.
BF 1031.P7923 1987   133.8   87-10209
ISBN 0-8094-6308-3
ISBN 0-8094-6309-1 (lib. bdg.)